I0817049

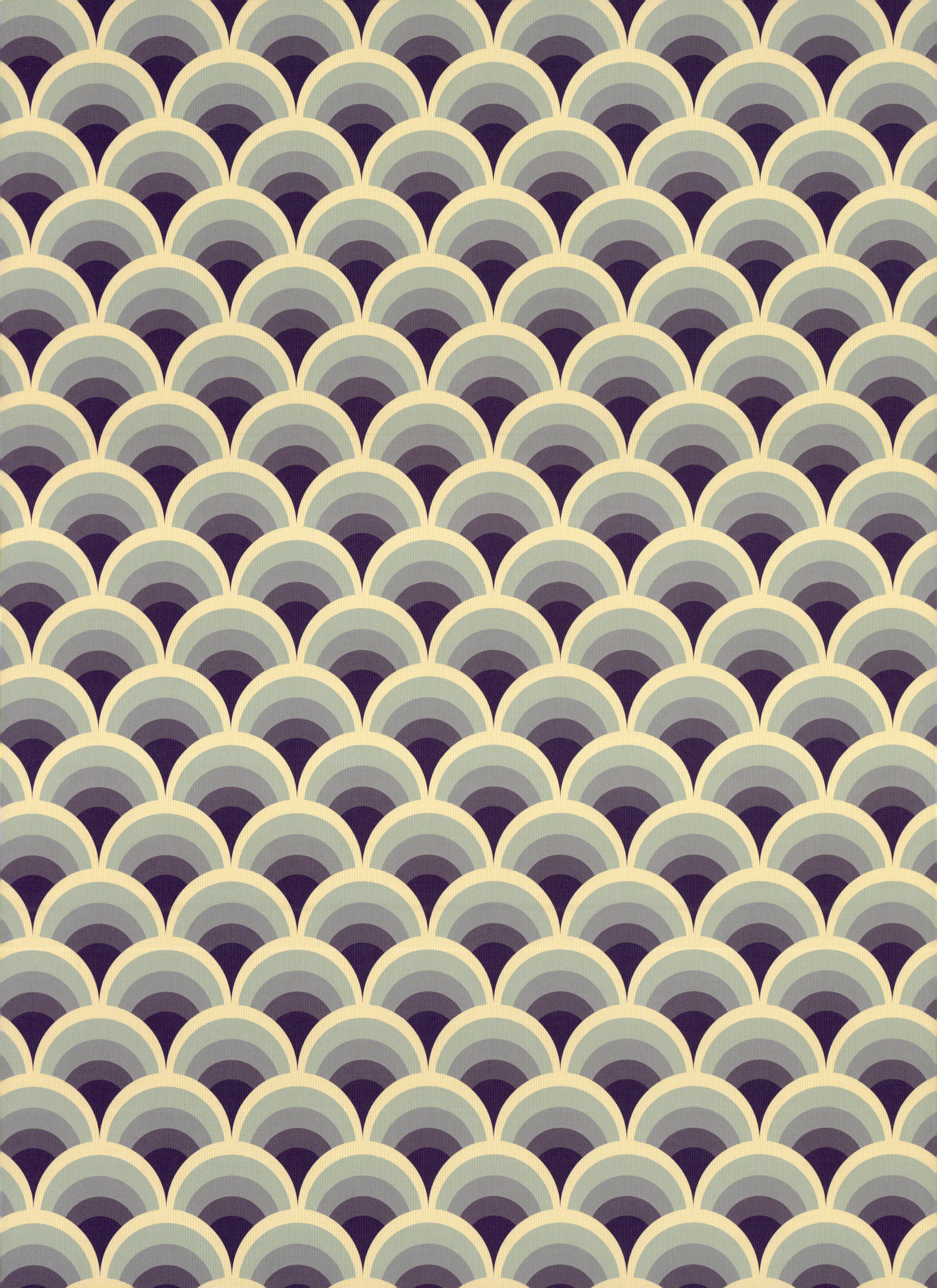

EVERY WAY with Granny Crochet

50 shapes in classic granny stitch

Julia Madill

DAVID & CHARLES
— PUBLISHING —

www.davidandcharles.com

Contents

Welcome

The inspiration for this book was born out of necessity: I wanted to own this book. I was minding my own beeswax designing a granny square vest when I found myself needing a new shape, a non-square shape, to create the perfect fit. I began looking for a reference book outlining all the different shapes you can make using the granny square stitch. The book's concept seemed so obvious to me, I was sure it had to exist. As it turns out, it didn't. So, I wrote it.

The granny square pattern is popular for many reasons: it's quick, simple, easy to memorize and easy to customize. I tried my best to carry these qualities forward when re-shaping this stitch into circles, stars, triangles and beyond. What's more, you'll find instructions to re-size most of these shapes so you can crochet teeny-tiny ornaments or epic afghans!

Don't know where to start? How to end? I've got the granny basics covered for you too, with all the info to take you from first loop to fabulous finishing. Many of the granny shapes fit together just like puzzle pieces so check out the "pairings" suggestions with each pattern. Want to see the shapes in action? The Sampler blanket combines a whole whack of shapes, borders and techniques.

You might think after a year-long exploration of the stitch I might not want to ever granny-square again; au contraire! Now that I've figured out all of these gran-tastic shapes, I want to put them to use in fun new designs! I hope these pages spark your imagination too.

Keep it crafty,

Julia

The Basics

Start Me Up

BEGINNING YOUR GRANNY JOURNEY

LET'S GET KNOTTY: THE SLIP KNOT

Typically the first step to get your yarn on your hook.

1. Create a loop with your yarn.
2. Bring the top strand under the loop.
3. Grab it with the hook and pull a loop through the first loop and onto the hook.
4. Gently tug both ends of yarn to tighten the resulting slip knot on the hook.

CHAIN-CHAIN-CHAIN: THE FOUNDATION CHAIN

Used as a base to work in rows.

1. Begin with a slip knot on your hook.
2. Yarn over hook and pull through the slip knot on the hook. This creates one chain.
3. Yarn over hook and pull through the loop on the hook. This creates one additional chain.
4. Repeat Step 3 to the desired number of chains.

YOU BETTER WERK: WORKING INTO THE FOUNDATION CHAIN

Stitches can be worked into the foundation chain in different ways. If unspecified in the pattern, choose the method that looks and feels right. Note you cannot work into the first chain from the hook (trust me, it doesn't work!). Your pattern will indicate where to begin working, but these illustrations show working into the second chain from the hook.

1. Work into the back loop only (easiest to work, least stable edge).
2. Work into the back loop as well as under the back bump.
3. Work into the top and bottom loops (hook is inserted into the back bump but with the top of the chain facing).
4. Work into the back bump only with the back of the chain facing (most difficult to work, most attractive edge).

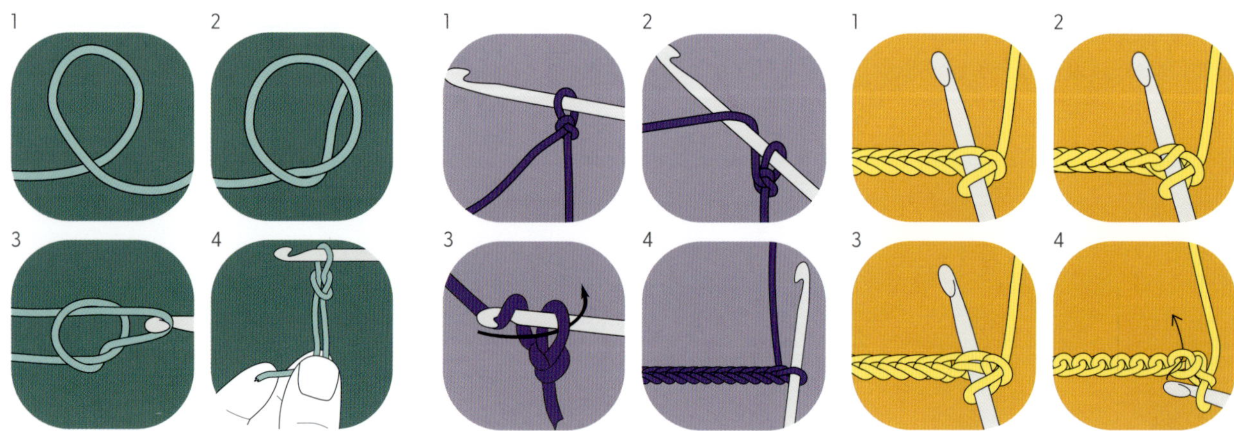

Good to know:

After making a magic ring, I count the chain created in Step 6 as the first chain in any starting chain required before working my first stitch into the ring. Not everyone does, and it doesn't make an enormous difference to the final result, so count your chains as you see fit.

RING ME UP: THE FOUNDATION RING

Used for working in rounds when the pattern begins with a tight circle of stitches. It can be used in place of the magic ring (I recommend a ring of 3 to 5 chains).

1. Begin with a slip knot on the hook and chain four or the number of chains indicated in the pattern.
2. Insert the hook into the first chain made (furthest from the hook) and join with a slip stitch (see Stitch Please! Basic Stitches) to form a ring, being careful not to twist the chain.
3. Work stitches into the space at the centre of the ring as indicated in the pattern.

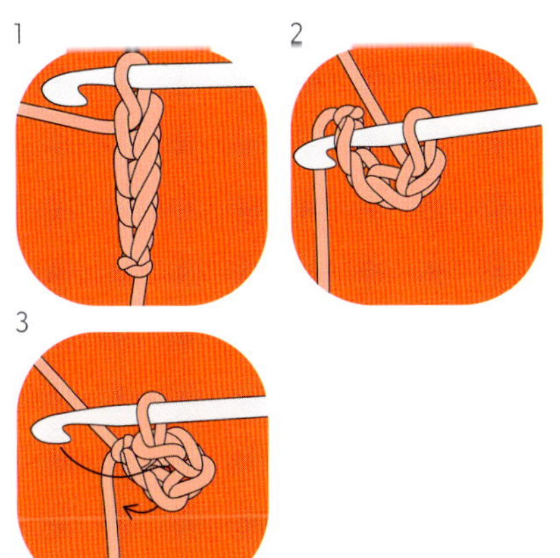

WOAH-OH-OH IT'S MAGIC! THE MAGIC RING

I suggest the magic ring (a.k.a. magic circle, adjustable ring or loop) to begin the shapes in this book worked in the round. It allows you to adjust the circumference of the ring easily and fully close the ring when complete.

1. Extend the first two fingers of your hand with palm facing. Place the tail end of yarn over your fingers and hold in place with your thumb.
2. Wrap the working yarn (coming from the ball) up, back and around your fingers once and then up, back and around once more, bringing it across the first to create an "X".
3. Turn your hand so that the back is facing. You will have two parallel strands of yarn across the back of your fingers. Insert your crochet hook under the strand closest to your fingertips, and hook the second strand.
4. Draw the second strand under the first, rotating your hook clockwise to twist the yarn and secure a loop on your hook.
5. Working over the first strand, hook the second strand again.
6. Draw the strand through the loop on your hook.
7. Pinch the base of the loop on the hook and gently remove the ring from your fingers.
8. Your magic ring is complete. Work any chains required prior to the first stitch of your round, then begin working stitches into the ring, working around both ring and yarn tail. When your first round is complete, pull the yarn tail to tighten the ring as desired.

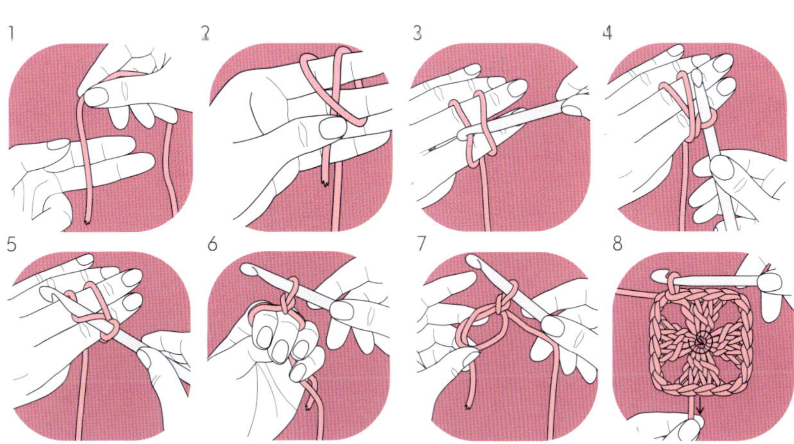

Keeping It Brief

ABBREVIATIONS

This book uses U.S. crochet terminology throughout.

Abbreviations

- beg = begin(ning)
- ch = chain(s)
- CL = cluster
- dc = double crochet
- hdc = half double crochet
- PM = place marker
- prev = previous
- rep = repeat
- rnd = round
- RS = right side
- sc = single crochet
- sk = skip
- sl st = slip stitch
- sp(s) = space(s)
- st(s) = stitch(es)
- tr = treble crochet
- WS = wrong side

"Ch 1" is an action direction, telling you make a one stitch chain

"Ch-1" is a thing, a reference to a previously made chain of one

Instructions within brackets [ ] should be worked in the st/sp indicated, or repeated the number of times stated immediately following the brackets.

In some instances, a smaller set of instructions needs to be repeated within a larger repeat. In this case, the smaller repeat will be indicated with parentheses ( ) within the larger instruction indicated with brackets [ ].

Repeated instructions may also be indicated with *. In these instances, the * indicates the beginning of the repeat and every instruction from the * to "rep from * to..." should be repeated.

Stitch, Please!

BASIC STITCHES

LET IT SLIP: SLIP STITCH (SL ST)

Commonly used to join rounds, this flat stitch usually isn't counted as a stitch at all.

1. Insert the hook into the indicated space, yarn over hook.
2. Pull the yarn through the work and the loop on the hook.

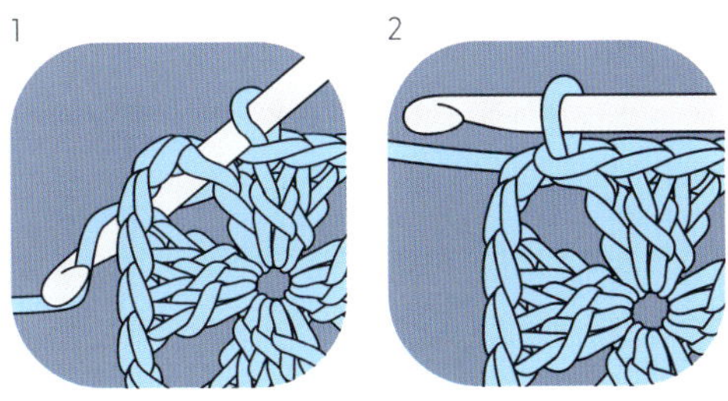

CHAIN REACTION: CHAIN STITCH (CH)

Commonly used to make spaces in your work and one of the two stitches required for the granny stitch.

1. Yarn over hook and pull through the loop on the hook (the hook is not inserted into a space).

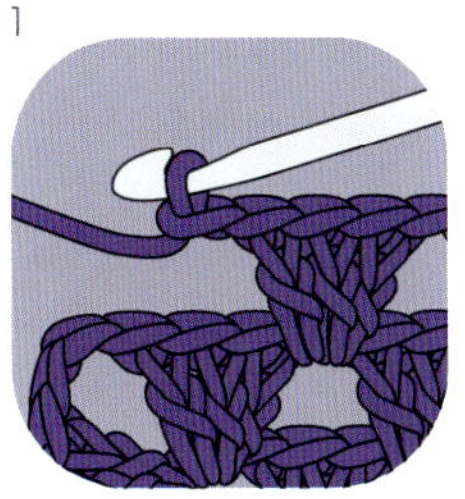

SINGLE AND LOVING IT: SINGLE CROCHET (SC)

This shorty-stitch creates a nice, dense fabric suitable for projects that require stability.

1. Insert the hook into the indicated space.
2. Yarn over and draw up a loop (two loops on hook), yarn over hook.
3. Pull through both loops on the hook to complete the stitch.

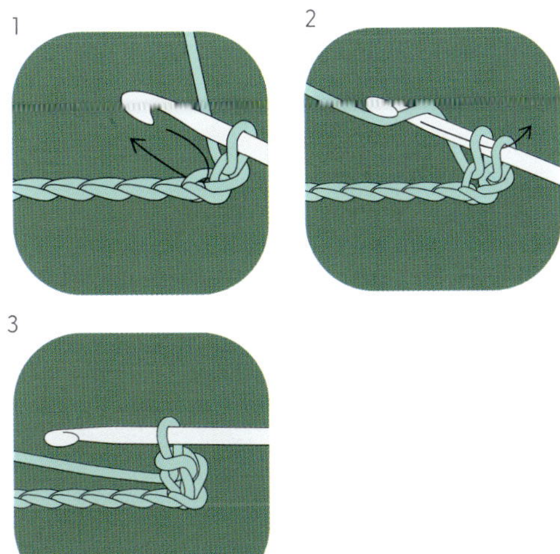

LET'S GO HALVSIES: HALF DOUBLE CROCHET (HDC)

Splitting the difference, this stitch is taller and more flexible than single and shorter and denser than double.

1. Yarn over and insert the hook into the indicated space.
2. Yarn over and draw up a loop (three loops on hook), yarn over.
3. Pull through three loops on the hook to complete the stitch.

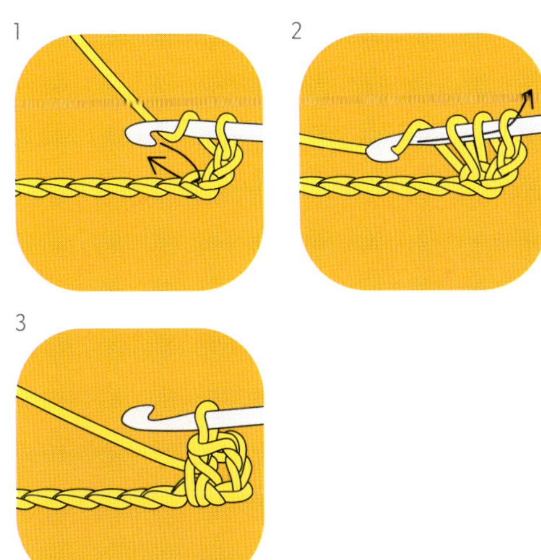

MAKE IT A DOUBLE: DOUBLE CROCHET (DC)

The queen-bee (or queen D?) of the granny stitch, this stitch has great flexibility while still retaining structure.

1. Yarn over hook and insert the hook into the indicated space.
2. Yarn over and draw up a loop (three loops on hook), yarn over hook.
3. Pull through the first two loops on the hook (two loops on hook), yarn over hook again.
4. Finally, pull through the last two loops on the hook to complete the stitch.

TRIPLE THREAT: TREBLE CROCHET (TR)

This tall drink of water is worked much the same way as the double crochet stitch, beginning with one extra yarn over. This stitch will grow your fabric quickly and has a lot of drape.

1. Yarn over hook twice and insert the hook into the indicated space.
2. Yarn over and draw up a loop (four loops on hook).
3. Yarn over and pull through the first two loops on the hook (three loops on hook).
4. Yarn over and pull through the next two loops on the hook (two loops on hook).
5. Yarn over and pull through the last two loops on the hook to complete the stitch.

Gran-tastic Beginnings

ALTERNATE STARTS

Good to know:

The most common way to begin a granny stitch round or row is with a chain of three stand-in for the first double crochet. Not satisfied with a chain masquerading as a stitch? Try one of these alternatives.

UNCHAINED: CHAINLESS BEGINNING DOUBLE CROCHET

An alternative to the ch-3 at the beginning of a row or round. This stitch more closely resembles a double crochet than a chain does, but requires some practice. Begin with a loop already on the hook and at the point when you are ready to begin a new row or round.

1. Draw the loop on the hook up to the height of a double crochet stitch. Holding the loop securely in place with a finger, twist the hook round to the right and behind the extended loop.
2. This creates a second loop on the hook. Still holding the original loop on the hook in place, insert the hook into the indicated space.
3. Yarn over hook and draw up a loop (three loops on hook).
4. Yarn over and pull through the first two loops on the hook (two loops on hook), yarn over again.
5. Pull through the last two loops on the hook to complete the stitch.

GET UP, STAND UP! STANDING DOUBLE CROCHET

Another great alternative to a ch-3 start, this double crochet variation is used when joining a new yarn.

1. Begin with a slip knot on the hook. Holding the slip knot in place with finger, yarn over hook. Insert the hook into the indicated space.
2. Yarn over and draw up a loop (three loops on hook).
3. Yarn over and pull through the first two loops on the hook (two loops on hook).
4. Yarn over and pull through the last two loops on the hook.

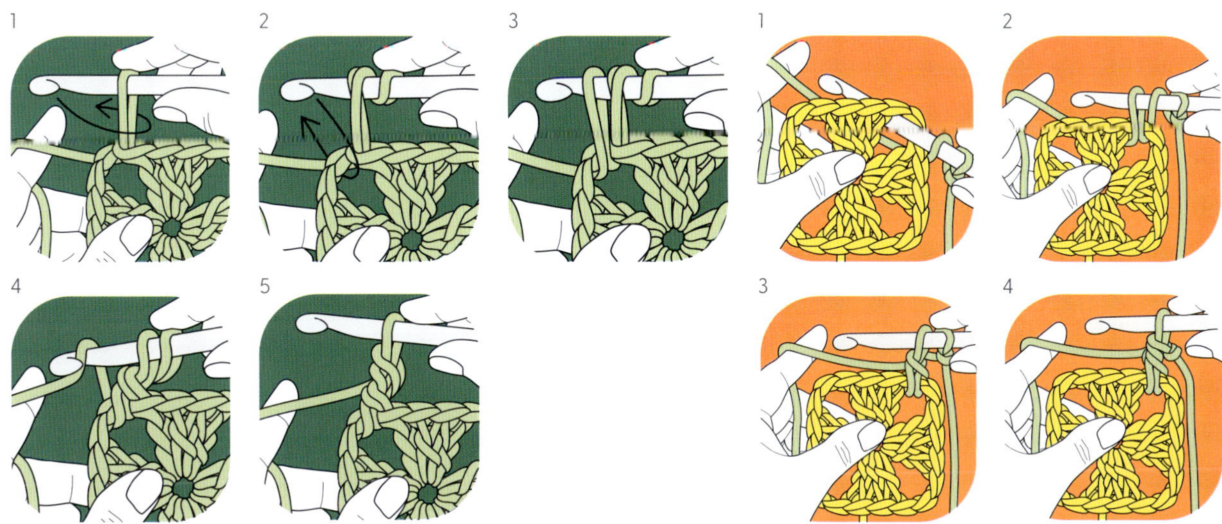

Gauge Old Wisdom

THE IMPORTANCE OF GAUGE

In crochet, gauge refers to the number of stitches and rows that fit within a specific measurement. Basically, it's the measure of the size of your stitches. Why should you care how big your stitches are? I'll give you three good reasons:

1. Gauge affects finished measurements. When following patterns, if you don't meet the quoted gauge, your project won't match the intended size.

#2. Gauge affects fabric. A too-loose gauge can give you a floppy, sloppy looking fabric. A too-tight gauge can make your fabric stiff.

#3. Gauge affects yarn requirements. A one-ball crochet project sounds great but if you don't meet the pattern-specified gauge, you may find yourself heading back to the yarn store before you're finished.

As this book is essentially a stitch dictionary, gauge concerns #1 and #3 don't really apply but are crucial to good results when following a project pattern. While most of the shapes in this book can be made to any size regardless of gauge, reason #2 still applies and you may want to adjust your gauge to create a suitable fabric for your project.

MEASURING UP: HOW TO CHECK YOUR GAUGE

Most crocheters seem positively allergic to making gauge swatches, but I highly recommend them if you are following a pattern and want good results.

Most pattern gauge is listed as number of stitches and rows per 10cm/4in, e.g. 20 sts and 8 rows = 10cm/4in.

Patchwork-style projects where you are joining squares or shapes often provide gauge as: 1 square = 15cm/6in.

- It's important to work your gauge swatch in the same yarn, stitch pattern and with the same hook that you intend to crochet your final project with.
- If you plan on blocking your final project, make sure to block your swatch before measuring.
- Measure your swatch on a smooth flat surface, and with a rigid ruler (not a flexible tape measure) to avoid distorting your measurement reading.
- Ensure your ruler aligns evenly with a row of stitches before counting.
- Measure in more than one place across the centre of your swatch, avoiding edges, to get a good average.
- Make your swatch a few stitches and rows larger than the gauge measurement provided. For example, if your gauge is listed as 10 dc and 5 rows = 10cm/4in, make a swatch at least 12 dc and 7 rows (larger is better). Edge stitches are often slightly distorted and should be avoided when measuring.

GRANNY GAUGE: GRANNY VS THE WORLD OF STITCHES

Granny gauge will match quite closely to a double-crochet fabric, but those chain spaces DO make a difference: granny stitch will typically be narrower horizontally than double crochet.

MAKING IT WORK: ADJUSTING GAUGE

The easiest and most effective way to adjust the gauge of your crochet is to change your hook size:

* Is your granny square stiff as a board? Are you getting more stitches per cm/in than your pattern calls for? Your gauge is too tight! Try going up a hook size or two.
* Is your granny square limp and loose? Do you have less stitches per cm/in than your pattern gauge calls for? Try going down a hook size.

These other factors can affect gauge and might be worth looking into:

* Hook hold: Do you grip your hook like a pencil or a knife?
* Hook material: You may find you work slightly differently when using a metal, wood or plastic hook.
* Yarn choice: Some yarns just don't want to meet your target gauge no matter what adjustments you make. If you're attempting to substitute dishcloth cotton for lace-weight mohair, you're trying to fit a square peg in a round hole, my friend.
* Mood and environment: Yep, you may not want to admit it, but the stitches you work poolside with a margarita and the ones you work while binge-watching horror movies can vary greatly in size and shape!

Taking Sides

THE RIGHT & THE WRONG SIDES

Good to know:
Most crochet patterns have a generally agreed upon "right" side and "wrong" side. While you may not agree with the predetermined "right" side of your work, what matters is that you can recognize the difference between the front and back of your stitches in order to control the look of your crochet fabric.

WORKING IN ROUNDS

The Classic Granny square, worked in the round, looks pretty similar on both sides, but the typical "right" side is the one that faces you as you crochet. The same side of the work is always facing when you work in the round so you will always be looking at the same side of each stitch. Can you tell the difference?

WORKING IN ROWS

When working in rows, you typically alternate which side is facing each row. In this case, the "right" and "wrong" side are both showing no matter which side you're looking at, so I consider these pieces to be reversible. That said, sometimes a side needs to be labelled RS/WS for reference purposes within the pattern instructions. In general, I prefer to make the right side the side that was facing when the last row or round was worked, as I prefer the look.

Turn It Up!

JOIN-&-TURN ROUNDS

WHY?

While the standard granny square looks almost identical on both sides, it isn't truly reversible if worked with the same side facing each time, because the stitches will look slightly different on each side. Want a more reversible look? There is a solution! By joining and turning your work at the end of each round, the "right" and "wrong" side will alternate and true reversibility is achieved. Huzzah!

Joining and turning rounds will also counteract the gradual shift that naturally occurs at the beginning of each round. If you've ever noticed a diagonal seam where your rounds are joined, that's because crochet stitches just don't line up vertically.

Turning at the end of each round alternates the direction of that diagonal shift and corrects the slant. Turning each round can also help avoid cutting and joining new yarn in some colour-work patterns. The Diagonal Half & Half Square and Quad Colour Square (seen below) would be much more fussy to work in standard rounds.

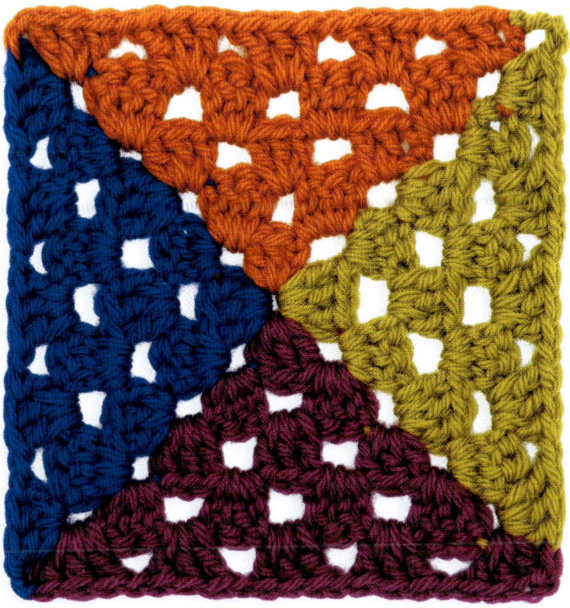

HOW?

Any shape in this book worked in rounds can be worked with join-&-turn rounds. The specifics of how to join-&-turn will depend on where and how your round is joined, but the basic concept is the same: join your round to complete it, turn the work, and work your next round with the opposite side facing. This may require an extra slip stitch at the beginning of the round to get you in the right position to work the first stitch.

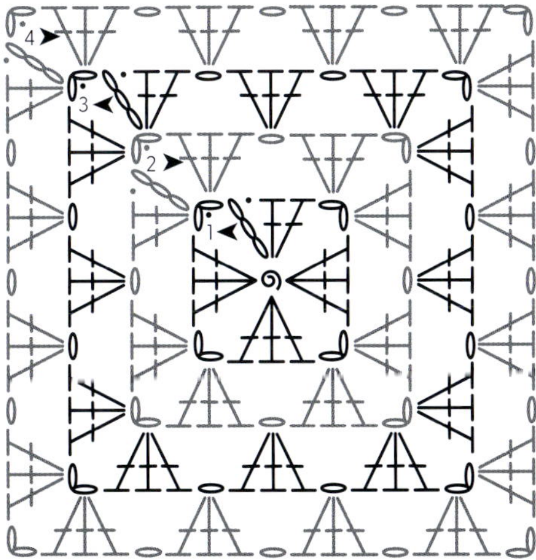

The stitch diagram shown here shows how the Classic Granny Version 1 would be converted to join-&-turn rounds. Note that odd-numbered rows are read counter-clockwise and even rows are read clockwise.

Chart Smarts
UNDERSTANDING CROCHET DIAGRAMS

WHERE TO START?

Each row or round in the diagram is numbered. The number will be found next to the first stitch (or chain etc) of the row/round.

WHAT DO THE SYMBOLS MEAN?

Each symbol in your diagram represents a stitch and the placement of the symbol represents where to work that stitch. The symbols used in crochet diagrams may vary in appearance from source to source, but the basic stitch symbols are fairly universal. Any diagram should be accompanied by a key to decipher its specific symbols. To decipher the symbols used for all the chart diagrams in this book, see the Symbol Key.

WHAT DO SYMBOLS IN DIFFERENT COLOURS MEAN?

It's fairly common to see crochet symbols shown in a different colour for each row or round in a chart. This is usually to make the chart easier to read and does not dictate a colour change unless otherwise specified in the pattern.

Good to know:

A visual representation of crochet stitches, diagrams have the advantage of being unconstrained by language. Once you become familiar with the basic stitch symbols, diagrams are a cinch to follow. All of the text patterns in this book are accompanied by a diagram.

WHICH WAY DO I GO?

The direction a stitch diagram is read varies depending on the direction the pattern is crocheted (see Sample Charts A, B and C).

SAMPLE CHART A: When working in rounds such as for many of the motifs in this book, a diagram is read from the centre out, with each round followed counter-clockwise (the direction that you would crochet the round if right-handed). The right side is always facing when working in the round so there is no need to switch directions such as when working in rows unless the specific pattern dictates.

SAMPLE CHART B: When working in rows, a diagram is generally read from bottom to top. An important thing to note is that diagrams show the pattern as it appears from just one side - the right side. This means right-side rows are read right to left (the direction you would crochet the row if right-handed) and wrong side rows are read left to right. This can be a tricky thing to get used to if new to reading diagrams but the placement of the row numbers are usually a good reminder. The charts in this book feature a direction indicator arrow beside each row/round number.

SAMPLE CHART C: When working in the round to create a tube, crochet diagrams typically show a reduced portion of the entire round and each round is read from right to left.

A

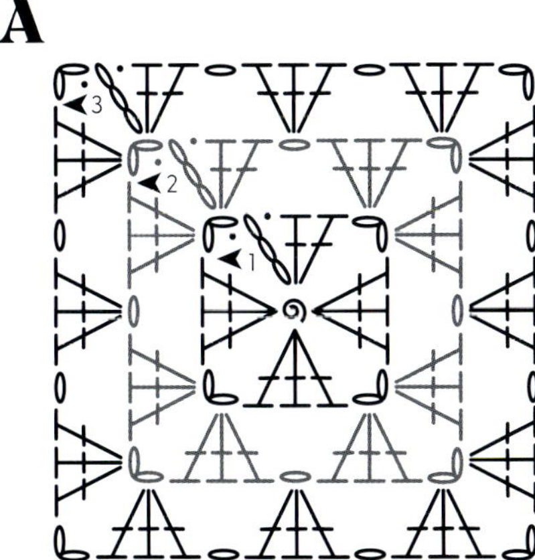

A chart showing a shape worked in rounds from the centre out. The numbers and arrows indicate where to start and which direction to work. The symbols are shown in black or grey on alternate rounds for legibility.

B

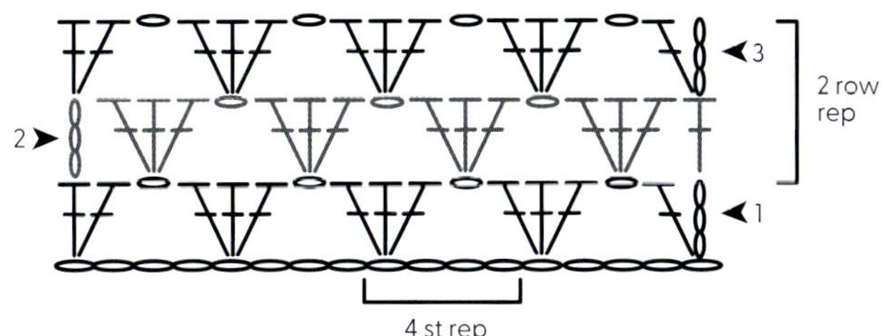

A chart showing a pattern worked in rows. The row numbers and direction arrows are shown at the first stitch of each row. A bracket at the bottom indicates the stitch repeat: the number of stitches to add or subtract to adjust the width of your work. The bracket at the right indicates the row repeat: the number of rows you need to repeat to adjust the length of your work. Which specific rows are repeated are indicated by the bracket.

Symbol Key

- Magic circle
- slip st (sl st)
- chain (ch)
- single crochet (sc)
- reverse sc
- half double crochet (hdc)
- double crochet (dc)
- dc2tog
- treble crochet (tr)

The key for all the crochet charts in this book, indicating what stitch is represented by what symbol.

C

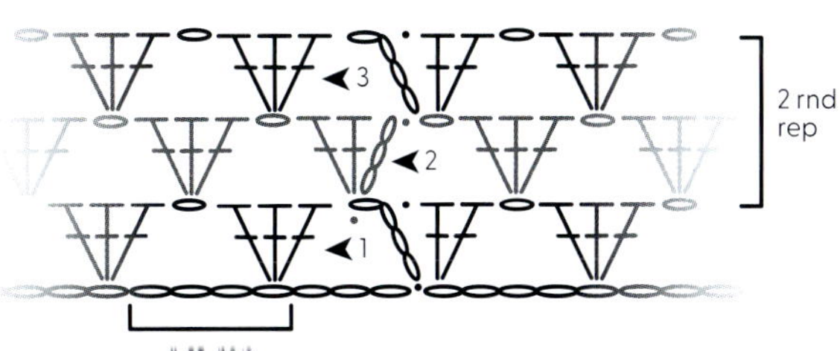

A chart showing a pattern worked in the round in a three-dimensional tube. Only a reduced segment of the work is shown, focusing on what needs to be repeated and how each round begins and ends.

Flying colours

USING COLOUR

Neutral

Kitschy classic

CHANGING COLOURS

The patterns in this book are written without colour changes indicated, providing a blank canvas for you to colour your own way. When you're ready to switch up your shades, here are three basic ways to do it:

#1 Fasten off: Fasten off and cut the old colour. Join the new colour with a slip stitch in the stitch or space where you need the first stitch of the new colour to begin. This simple finish-and-start-again move is what you would generally use when working in rows, although it works for almost any colour-change situation.

#2 Joining the round: Use the new colour for the joining slip stitch at the end of a round. Cut the old colour and proceed with the new. Applicable to working in rounds only, this technique simultaneously finishes your round with the old colour and leaves you with the new colour on your hook, ready to go.

#3 Joining to stitch: Finish the last stitch of the old colour by working to the last two loops on the hook, yarn over with the new colour and pull through the last loops, completing the stitch. Cut the old colour and proceed with the new. This is your move if you want to change colours in the middle of row or round.

CHOOSING COLOURS

Colour is transformative. The same crochet pattern made in different colour combinations can have a radically different look and feel. Imagine the bright multi-hued granny afghan we all know and love made in only neutral shades? The kitschy classic is suddenly transformed to refined, minimalist, high-end decor.

Choosing colours for a crochet project might be your favourite day at the yarn store, or an anxiety-inducing chore depending on your relationship with colour. No matter how you feel about it, here are a few things I've learned along the way that might help you on your colour journey.

CAST YOUR CONTRAST

Some designs need highly contrasting shades in order for the pattern to read. Take the Circle in a Square pattern as an example: to see the circle, you need it to pop against the background. Or maybe you want that circle to be a subtle detail? In that case, choose two similar shades and let that circle lay low.

Good to know:

When carrying colours up rows/rounds, it may make more sense to simply leave the old colour hanging out in back while you work with the new colour, then pick it up again when you need it (join #2 is great in this situation). This works best if the old colour is carried up for only one or two rows/rounds as it will leave a visible "float" or strand of yarn at the back or side of your work. On the upside, carrying up colour this way can save you weaving in a million ends!

Low contrast

High contrast

INTENSE VALUE

I like to think that shades with similar levels of saturation (intensity) and value (lightness or darkness) belong in the same "family". Think of a selection of soft pastels, or day-glow neons. Matching the saturation and intensity of your colour choices usually creates a palette of shades that look like they belong together. I won't tell you to never mix your pastels and neons (it can yield so super-cool results) but proceed with caution!

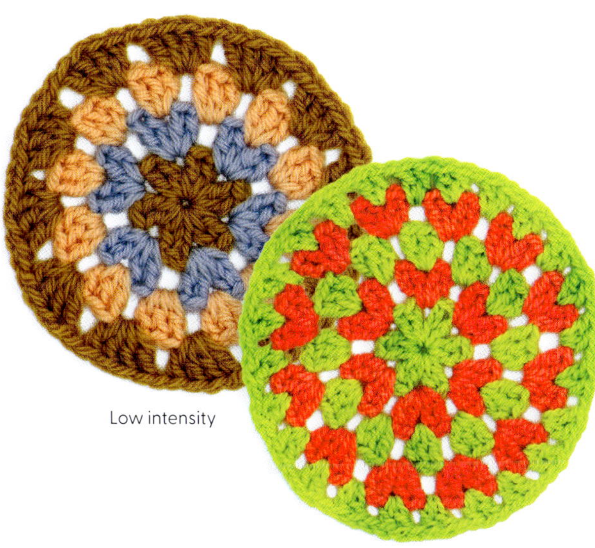

Low intensity

High intensity

DON'T REINVENT THE WHEEL

No mention of colour theory would be complete without our old friend: the colour wheel. If you're lacking inspiration, play around with some of the traditional colour combinations you can build with this simple tool:

* Monochromatic: One colour from the wheel split into different values (for example, light pink, medium pink, dark pink)
* Analogous: Adjacent colours on the wheel (such as red, magenta)
* Triadic: Three equally-spaced colours on the wheel (such as red, yellow, blue)
* Complementary: Two colours opposite each other on the wheel (such as orange, blue)
* Split Complementary: One colour combined with the two shades on either side of its complement (such as blue, red-orange, yellow-orange)

COPY AND PASTE

Some of the best colour combos I've put together have been borrowed from items that have nothing to do with yarn: a wallpaper print, a peacock feather, vintage pyrex bowls, that pile of LEGO® my kid left on the floor. Colour inspiration is everywhere!

Colour combo inspired by LEGO®

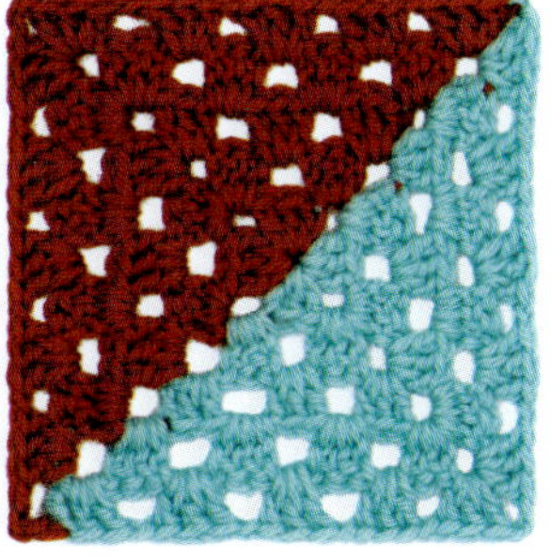

Complementary

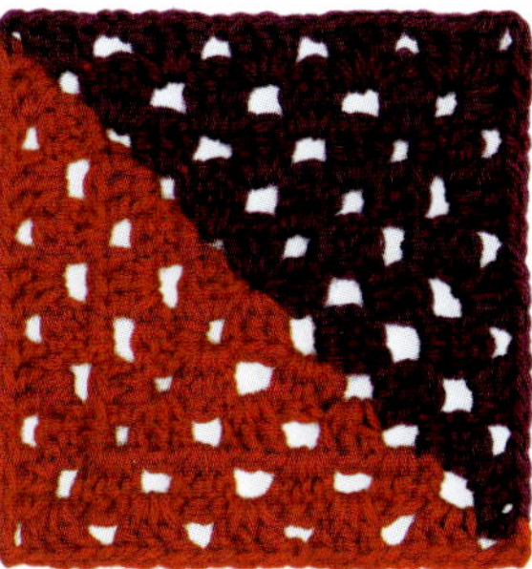

Analogous

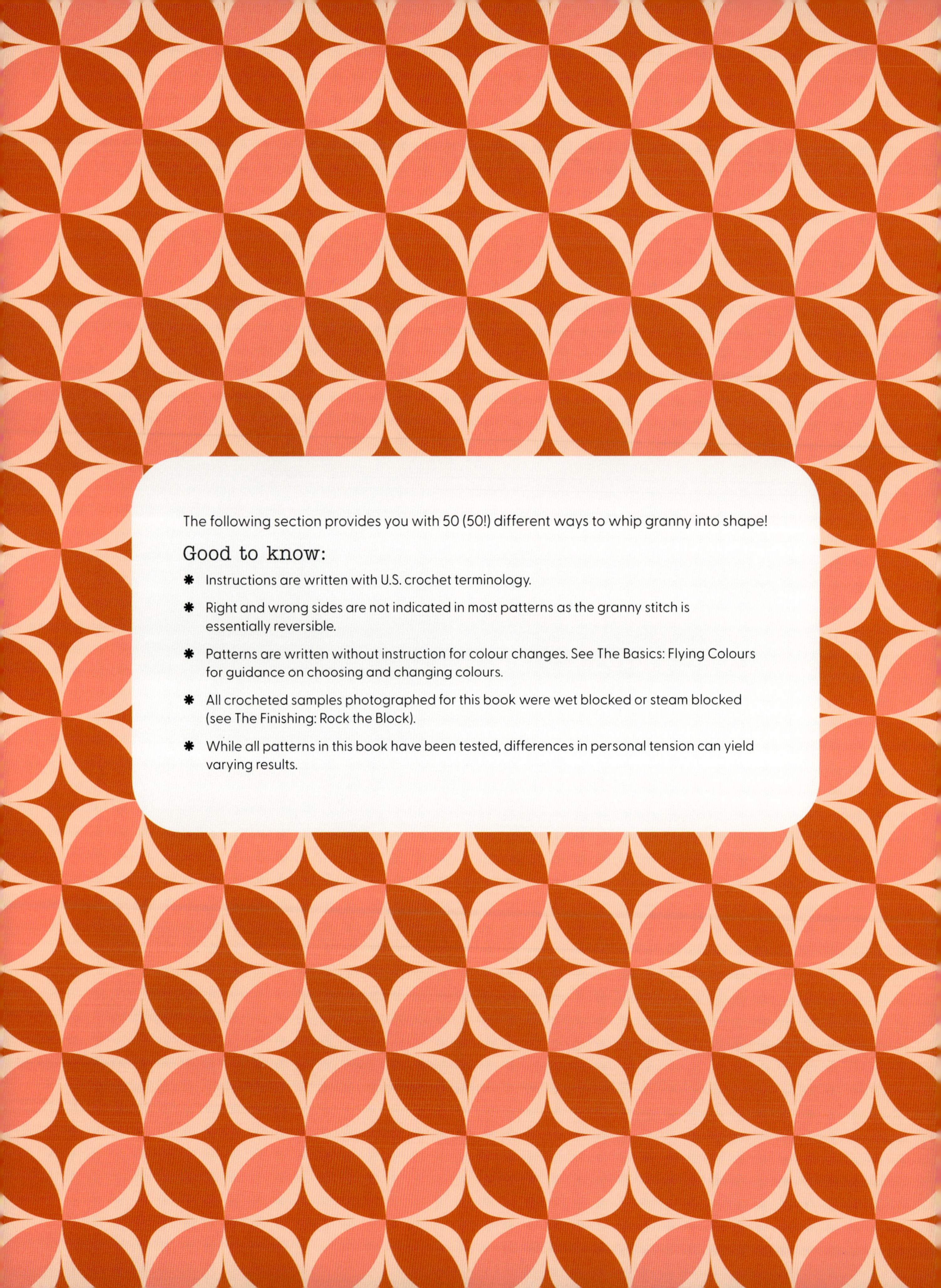

The following section provides you with 50 (50!) different ways to whip granny into shape!

Good to know:

- Instructions are written with U.S. crochet terminology.
- Right and wrong sides are not indicated in most patterns as the granny stitch is essentially reversible.
- Patterns are written without instruction for colour changes. See The Basics: Flying Colours for guidance on choosing and changing colours.
- All crocheted samples photographed for this book were wet blocked or steam blocked (see The Finishing: Rock the Block).
- While all patterns in this book have been tested, differences in personal tension can yield varying results.

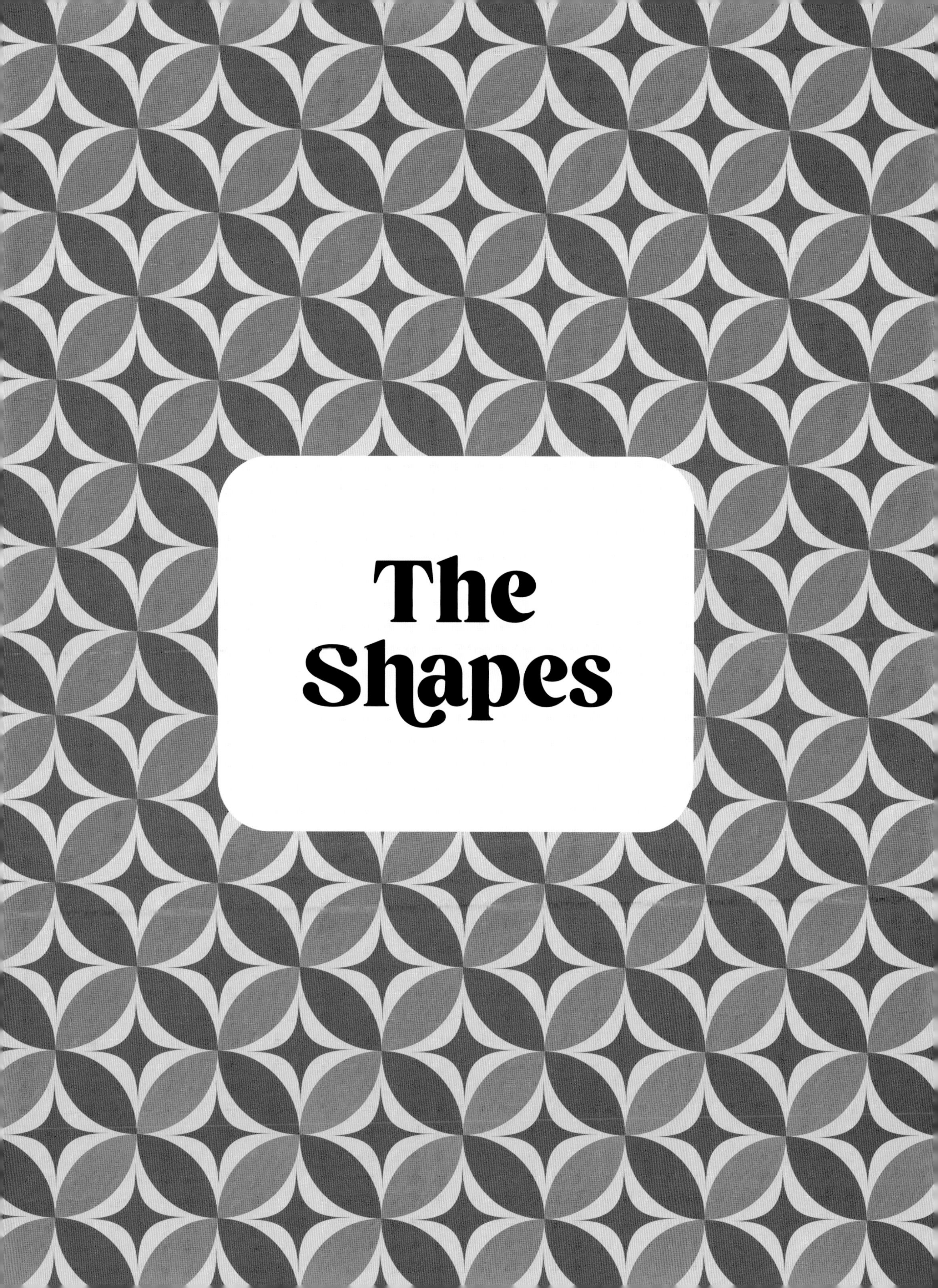

The Shapes

Granny #01

Classic Granny

This is the O.G. (Original Granny, naturally). Instantly recognizable, this pervasive crochet square is a classic for good reason: it's easy to work, quick to memorize, effortlessly re-sized, attractive and versatile. Just like I had a Granny and you may have an Oma or a Bubbe, there are slight variations of the Classic Granny square, and each has its own unique charms.

VERSIONS 1, 2, 3 & 4

These are all worked in rounds with the right side facing at all times. The difference between the four options is where and how the beginning of each round is treated.

VERSION 1: CORNER JOIN

This is my personal, go-to granny. It finishes at the corner, allowing you to leave your last yarn tail in an ideal spot for seaming.

Best for:

Positioning yarn tails at corners for seaming

Instructions

Make magic ring.

First rnd: Ch 5 (counts as 1 dc, ch-2 sp throughout), [3 dc, ch 2] 3 times in ring, 2 dc in ring, join with sl st to 3rd ch of beg ch-5.

2nd rnd: Sl st in first ch-2 sp, ch 5, 3 dc in same ch-2 sp, ch 1, [(3 dc, ch 2, 3 dc) in next ch-2 sp, ch 1] 3 times, 2 dc in first ch-2 sp, join with sl st to 3rd ch of beg ch-5.

3rd rnd: Sl st in first ch-2 sp, ch 5, 3 dc in same ch-2 sp, [ch 1, 3 dc in next ch-1 sp, ch 1, (3 dc, ch 2, 3 dc) in next ch-2 sp] 3 times, ch 1, 3 dc in next ch-1 sp, ch 1, 2 dc in first ch-2 sp, join with sl st to 3rd ch of beg ch-5.

4th rnd: Sl st in first ch-2 sp, ch 5, 3 dc in same ch-2 sp, ch 1, [(3 dc, ch 1) in each ch-1 sp to next corner ch-2 sp, (3 dc, ch 2, 3 dc) in corner ch-2 sp, ch 1] 3 times, [3 dc, ch 1] in each ch-1 sp to first corner ch-2 sp, 2 dc in first corner ch-2 sp, join with sl st to 3rd ch of beg ch-5.

To Modify

- Rep 4th rnd to desired size.
- If changing colours at beg of each rnd, join new colour with sl st at any corner ch-2 sp. Then skip the first sl st and begin the new rnd with ch 5.

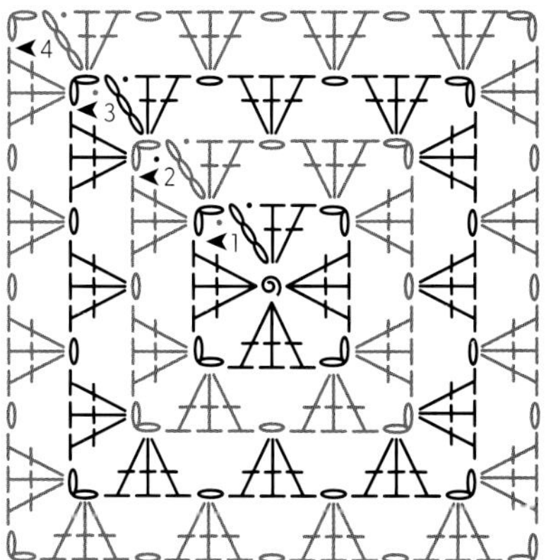

VERSION 2: SIDE JOIN

For the most part, the difference between Version 1 and Version 2 is a po-TAY-to, po-TAH-to situation: choose which feels right for you.

Best for:

Positioning end of rnd at centre side

Instructions

Make magic ring.

First rnd: Ch 3 (counts as 1 dc throughout), 2 dc in ring, ch 2, [3 dc, ch 2] 3 times in ring, join with sl st in top of beg ch-3.

2nd rnd: Ch 4 (counts as 1 dc, ch-1 sp throughout), [(3 dc, ch 2, 3 dc) in next ch-2 sp, ch 1] 3 times, [3 dc, ch 3, 2 dc] in last ch-2 sp, join with sl st to 3rd ch of beg ch-4.

3rd rnd: Sl st in first ch-1 sp, ch 3, 2 dc in same ch-1 sp, ch 1, [(3 dc, ch 2, 3 dc) in next ch-2 sp, ch 1, 3 dc in next ch-1 sp, ch 1] 3 times, [3 dc, ch 2, 3 dc] in last ch-2 sp, ch 1, join with sl st in top of beg ch-3.

4th rnd: Ch 4, [(3 dc, ch 1) in each ch-1 sp to next corner ch-2 sp, (3 dc, ch 2, 3 dc) in corner ch-2 sp, ch 1] 4 times, 2 dc in next ch-1 sp, join with sl st to 3rd ch of beg ch-4.

5th rnd: Sl st in first ch-1 sp, ch 3, 2 dc in same ch-1 sp, ch 1, [(3 dc, ch 1) in each ch-1 sp to next corner ch-2 sp, (3 dc, ch 2, 3 dc) in next corner ch-2 sp, ch 1] 4 times, [3 dc, ch 1] in each ch-1 sp around, join with sl st in top of beg ch-3.

6th rnd: Ch 4, [(3 dc, ch 1) in each ch-1 sp to next corner ch-2 sp, (3 dc, ch 2, 3 dc) in corner ch-2 sp, ch 1] 4 times, [3 dc, ch 1] in each ch-1 sp to last ch-1 sp, 2 dc in last ch-1 sp, join with sl st to 3rd ch of beg ch-4.

To Modify

- Rep 5th and 6th rnd to desired size.
- If changing colours at beg of each rnd, join new colour with sl st to *last* ch-1 sp of prev round for even-numbered rnds and *first* ch-1 sp of prev rnd for odd-numbered rnds.

VERSION 3: SLIP STITCH CORNER

When I worked in a yarn store, a co-worker showed me this way of crocheting granny squares. Scootch-ing over to the corner with a bunch of slip stitches feels like cheating, but they are only necessary when you work in one colour. If joining a new colour each rnd, you can skip the slipped stitches and then this granny's not so off-her-rocker.

Best for:

Changing colours each rnd

Instructions

Make magic ring.

First rnd: Ch 3 (counts as 1 dc throughout), 2 dc in ring, ch 2, [3 dc, ch 2] 3 times in ring, join with sl st in top of beg ch-3.

2nd rnd: Sl st in each of first 2 dc and next ch-2 sp, *ch 3, [2 dc, ch 2, 3 dc] in same ch-2 sp, ch 1, [(3 dc, ch 2, 3 dc) in next ch-2 sp, ch-1] 3 times, join with sl st in top of beg ch-3.

3rd rnd: Sl st in each of first 2 dc and next ch-2 sp, *ch 3, [2 dc, ch 2, 3 dc] in same ch-2 sp, ch 1, 3 dc in next ch-1 sp, ch 1, [(3 dc, ch 2, 3 dc) in next ch-2 sp, ch 1, 3 dc in next ch-1 sp, ch 1] 3 times, join with sl st in top of beg ch-3.

4th rnd: Sl st in each of first 2 dc and next ch-2 sp, *ch 3, [2 dc, ch 2, 3 dc] in same ch-2 sp, ch 1, [3 dc, ch 1] in each ch-1 sp to next corner ch-2 sp, [(3 dc, ch 2, 3 dc) in corner ch-2 sp, ch 1, (3 dc, ch 1) in each ch-1 sp to next corner ch-2 sp] 3 times, join with sl st in top of beg ch-3.

To Modify

- Rep 4th rnd to desired size.
- If changing colour each rnd, join new colour with sl st at any corner ch-2 sp. Begin 2nd to 4th rnds at *, fasten off at end of each rnd.

VERSION 4: HALF DOUBLE CROCHET JOIN

This little variation allows you to begin and end your rounds right smack in the middle of a corner space.

Joining each round with a chain and an hdc positions your last stitch just right, eliminating the need to slip stitch over to the corner to begin your next round. Treat this "ch-1, hdc" like a regular ch-2 corner for subsequent rounds, working into the space not the hdc stitch itself.

Best for:

Working colour changes at corners (as seen in Diagonal Half & Half Square and Quad Colour Square)

Instructions

Make magic ring.

First rnd: Ch 3 (counts as 1 dc throughout), 2 dc in ring, [ch 2, 3 dc] 3 times in ring, ch 1, join with hdc in top of beg ch-3. (counts as corner ch-2 sp throughout)

2nd rnd: Ch 3, 2 dc in first corner sp, ch 1, [(3 dc, ch 2, 3 dc) in next ch-2 sp, ch 1] 3 times, 3 dc in first corner sp, ch 1, join with hdc in top of beg ch-3.

3rd rnd: Ch 3, 2 dc in first corner sp, [ch 1, 3 dc in next ch-1 sp, ch 1, (3 dc, ch 2, 3 dc) in next ch-2 sp] 3 times, ch 1, 3 dc in next ch-1 sp, ch 1, 3 dc in first corner sp, ch 1, join with hdc in top of beg ch-3.

4th rnd: Ch 3, 2 dc in same corner sp, ch 1, [(3 dc, ch 1) in each ch-1 sp to next corner ch-2 sp, (3 dc, ch 2, 3 dc) in corner ch-2 sp, ch 1] 3 times, [3 dc, ch 1] in each ch-1 sp to first corner sp, 3 dc in first corner sp, ch 1, join with hdc in top of beg ch-3.

To Modify

- Rep 4th rnd to desired size.
- If changing colours each rnd, join new colour when completing joining hdc st.

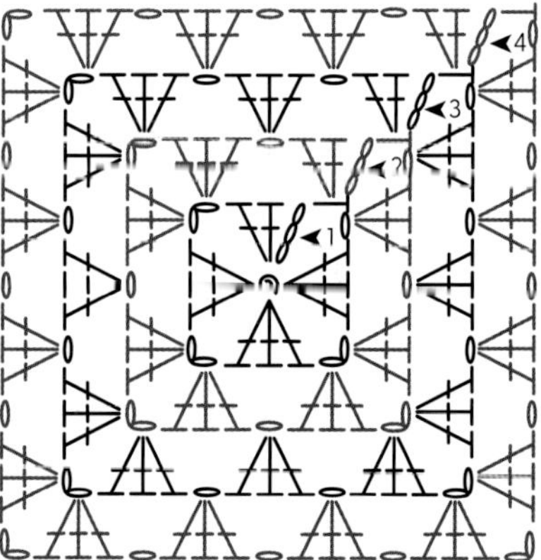

ALL VERSIONS

To Modify

- Working ch-3 instead of ch-2 in each corner is a common Classic Granny square variation. I prefer ch-2 so each chain can "belong" to one side of square. Ultimately, I don't find much difference between ch-2 and ch-3 corners so try both and choose what you prefer.
- Eliminating ch-1 sps at each side of square is another common Classic Granny square variation. In this case, stitches are simply worked into space between 3-dcCLs. This makes a slightly denser/tighter fabric which can be beneficial for projects that require structure.

The Stats

- Pairs well with Half Square Triangle 1 or 2, any rectangle, Boot

Version 1

Version 2

Version 3

Version 4

Note: Circle indicates the beginning of the round

Granny #02

Granny Stitch in Rows & Rounds

This is the granny stitch pattern at its essence and the basis for everything in this book. Worked in rows, the granny stitch can easily make a square or rectangle, or use the formula to add on to the sides of other shapes. It would be irresponsible of me to write about granny stitch without explaining how to work it in the round. Granny can get totally tubular too!

GRANNY STITCH IN ROWS

Instructions

Ch multiple of 4, minimum of 12.

First row: 1 dc in 4th ch from hook (skipped ch-3 counts as 1 dc), ch 1, sk next 3 ch, [3 dc in next ch, ch 1, sk next 3 ch] to last ch, 2 dc in last ch. Turn.

2nd row: Ch 3 (counts as 1 dc throughout), [3 dc, ch 1] in each ch-1 sp to last ch-1 sp, 3 dc in last ch-1 sp, 1 dc in top of ch-3. Turn.

3rd row: Ch 3, 1 dc in first dc, ch 1, [3 dc, ch1] in each ch-1 sp to end of row, 2 dc in top of ch-3. Turn.

To Modify

- Rep 2nd and 3rd rows to desired length.
- You can add granny rows to a Classic Granny square to elongate a side:

Join yarn with sl st to desired corner sp.

Add-on first row: Ch 3, 1 dc in same sp, ch 1, [3 dc, ch 1] in each ch-1 sp to next corner sp, 2 dc in corner sp. Turn.

Rep 2nd and 3rd rows to desired length.

The Stats

- Worked in rows
- Infinite growth potential
- Infinite proportion variations

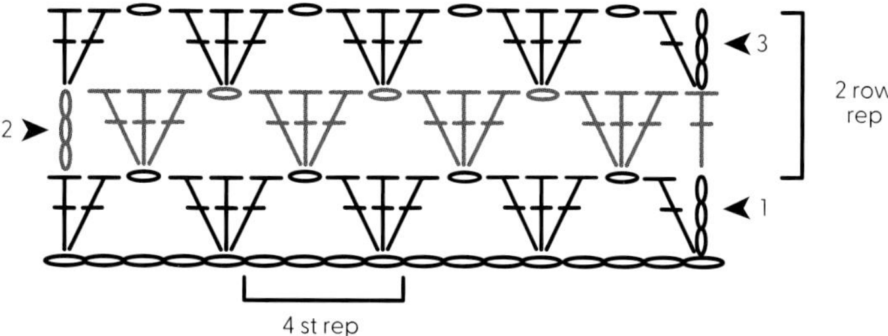

GRANNY STITCH IN ROUNDS

Instructions

Ch multiple of 4, minimum approx 16 (smaller number may create a tube too small to work with).

Being careful not to twist chain, join with sl st to first ch.

First rnd: Ch 3 (counts as 1 dc throughout), 2 dc in first ch, ch 1, sk next 3 ch, *3 dc in next ch, ch 1, sk next 3 ch, rep from * around, join with sl st in top of beg ch-3.

2nd rnd: Ch 4 (counts as 1 dc, ch-1 sp throughout), *3 dc in next ch-1 sp, ch 1; rep from * to last ch-1 sp, 2 dc in last ch-1 sp, join with sl st to 3rd ch of beg ch-4.

3rd rnd: Sl st in first ch-1 sp, ch 3, 2 dc in same sp, ch 1, *3 dc in next ch-1 sp, ch 1; rep from * around, join with sl st in top of beg ch-3.

To Modify

- Rep 2nd and 3rd rnds to desired length.
- Add or subtract 4 to foundation ch to create wider or narrower tube.

The Stats

- Worked in rnds
- Creates 3-dimensional tube
- Infinite growth potential
- Infinite proportion variations

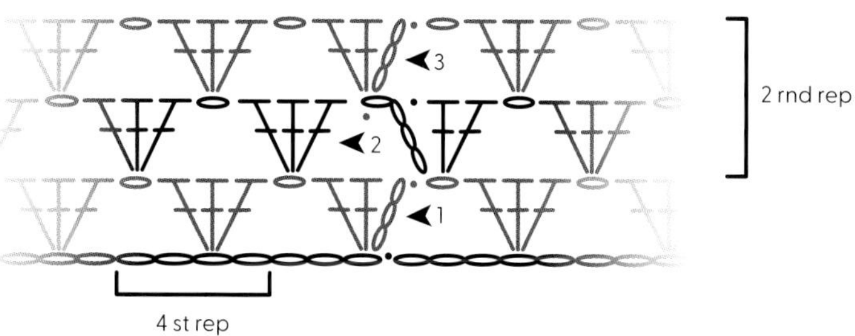

Granny #03

Diagonal Half & Half Square

Sometimes half the work of a crochet patchwork project is sewing all those pieces together, so why not cut that work in half? Not half bad, right? I love this square for giving the appearance of two triangles without any sewing. It's ideal for replicating traditional quilt patterns and a fun shape to use when playing around with colour.

Instructions

Notes:

* Do not cut yarn when changing colours but leave the colour not in use at WS of work: to the back on RS rows, to the front on WS rows).
* To change colours cleanly while creating ch-2 corners: ch 1 in old colour, draw new colour through loop on hook creating 2nd ch-1 in old colour and setting up new colour on hook.
* When picking up colours from the prev rnd, bring the new colour up to the height of the current rnd creating a vertical strand. This strand will blend in with the stitch next to it and is hardly noticeable in the finished square.

Using A, make magic ring.

First rnd (RS): Using A, ch 3 (counts as 1 dc throughout), [2 dc, ch 2, 3 dc, ch 2] in ring, using B, [3 dc, ch 2, 3 dc, ch 1] in ring, join with hdc in top of beg ch-3 (counts as ch-2 corner sp throughout). Turn.

2nd rnd (WS): Using B, ch 3, 2 dc in first corner sp, ch 1, [3 dc, ch 2, 3 dc] in next ch-2 sp, ch 1, 3 dc in next ch-2 sp, ch 2, using A, 3 dc in same ch-2 sp, ch 1, [3 dc, ch 2, 3 dc] in next ch-2 sp, ch 1, 3 dc in first corner sp, ch 1, join with hdc in top of beg ch-3 (counts as ch-2 corner sp throughout). Turn.

3rd rnd: Using A, ch 3, 2 dc in first corner sp, ch 1, 3 dc in next ch-1 sp, ch 1, [3 dc, ch 2, 3 dc] in next ch-2 sp, ch 1, 3 dc in next ch-1 sp, ch 1, 3 dc in next ch-2 sp, ch 2 joining B to last ch, using B, 3 dc in same ch-2 sp, ch 1, 3 dc in next ch-1 sp, ch 1, [3 dc, ch 2, 3 dc] in next ch-2 sp, ch 1, 3 dc in next ch-1 sp, ch 1, 3 dc in first corner sp, ch 1, join with hdc in top of beg ch-3. Turn.

4th rnd: Using B, ch 3, 2 dc in first corner sp, ch 1, [3 dc, ch 1] in each ch-1 sp to next corner ch-2 sp, [3 dc, ch 2, 3 dc] in next ch-2 sp, ch 1, [3 dc, ch 1] in each ch-1 sp to next corner ch-2 sp, ch 1, 3 dc in next ch-2 sp, ch 2 joining A to last ch, using A, 3 dc in same ch-2 sp, ch 1, [3 dc, ch 1] in each ch-1 sp to next corner ch-2 sp, [3 dc, ch 2, 3 dc] in next ch-2 sp, ch 1, [3 dc, ch 1] in each ch-1 sp to first corner ch-2 sp, 3 dc in first corner sp, ch 1, join with hdc in top of beg ch-3. Turn.

5th rnd: Rep 4th rnd, reversing references to A and B.Turn.

The Stats

* Worked in join-&-turn rnds
* Requires two colours
* Infinite growth potential
* Pairs well with any square or rectangle, Half Square Triangle 1

To Modify

* Repeat 4th and 5th rnds to desired size.
* To avoid contrast colour peeking through when working into corner ch-2 sps, use your fingers to slide first 3-dcCL in corner up close to same colour stitches beside it.

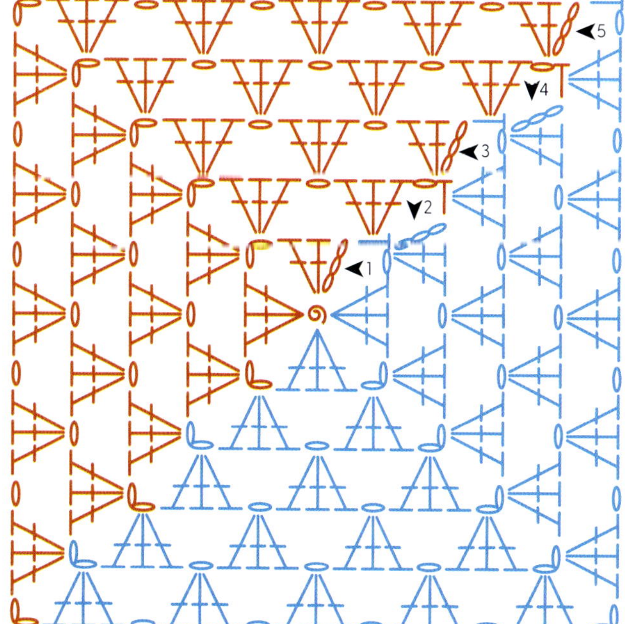

Granny #04

Quad Colour Square

Patchwork is dandy but colourwork is quicker (within reason). The Quad Colour Square appears to be four triangles patched together, but is actually your basic granny square with some clever shade-swapping. Four times the fun!

Instructions

Notes:

* Do not cut yarn when changing colours but leave the colour not in use at WS of work: to the back on RS rows, to the front on WS rows).
* To change colours cleanly while creating ch-2 corners: ch 1 in old colour, draw new colour through loop on hook creating 2nd ch-1 in old colour and setting up new colour on hook.
* When picking up colours from the prev rnd, bring the new colour up to the height of the current rnd creating a vertical strand. This strand will blend in with the stitch next to it and is hardly noticeable in the finished square.

Using A, make magic ring.

First rnd (RS): Using A, ch 3 (counts as 1 dc throughout), 2 dc in ring, ch 2, using B, 3 dc in ring, ch 2, using C, 3 dc in ring, ch 2, using D, 3 dc in ring, ch 1, join with hdc in top of ch-3 (counts as ch-2 corner sp throughout). Turn.

2nd rnd (WS): Using D, ch 3, 2 dc in first corner sp, ch 1, 3 dc in next ch-2 sp, ch 2, using C, 3 dc in same sp, ch 1, 3 dc in next ch-2 sp, ch 2, using B, 3 dc in same sp, ch 1, 3 dc in next ch-2 sp, ch 2, using A, 3 dc in same sp, ch 1, 3 dc in first corner sp, ch 1, join with hdc in top of beg ch-3. Turn.

3rd rnd: Using A, ch 3, 2 dc in first corner sp, ch 1, 3 dc in next ch-1 sp, ch 1, 3 dc in next ch-2 sp, ch 2, using B, 3 dc in same sp, ch 1, 3 dc in next ch-1 sp, ch 1, 3 dc in next ch-2 sp, ch 2, using C, 3 dc in same sp, ch 1, 3 dc in next ch-1 sp, ch 1, 3 dc in next ch-2 sp, ch 2, using D, 3 dc in same sp, ch 1, 3 dc in next ch-1 sp, ch 1, 3 dc in first corner sp, ch 1, join with hdc in top of beg ch-3. Turn.

4th rnd: Using D, ch 3, 2 dc in first corner sp, ch 1, [3 dc, ch 1] in each ch-1 sp to next ch-2 sp, 3 dc in next ch-2 sp, ch 2, using C, 3 dc in same sp, ch 1, [3 dc, ch 1] in each ch-1 sp to next ch-2 sp, 3 dc in next ch-2 sp, ch 2, using B, 3 dc in same sp, ch 1, [3 dc, ch 1] in each ch-1 sp to next ch-2 sp, 3 dc in next ch-2 sp, ch-2, using A, 3 dc in same sp, ch 1, [3 dc, ch-1] in each ch-1 sp to first ch-2 sp, 3 dc in first corner sp, ch 1, join with hdc in top of beg ch-3. Turn.

5th rnd: Using A, ch 3, 2 dc in first corner sp, ch 1, [3 dc, ch 1] in each ch-1 sp to next ch-2 sp, 3 dc in next ch-2 sp, ch 2, using B, 3 dc in same sp, ch 1, [3 dc, ch 1] in each ch-1 sp to next ch-2 sp, 3 dc in next ch-2 sp, ch 2, using C, 3 dc in same sp, ch 1, [3 dc, ch 1] in each ch-1 sp to next ch-2 sp, 3 dc in next ch-2 sp, ch 2, using D, 3 dc in same sp, ch 1, [3 dc, ch 1] in each ch-1 sp to first corner sp, 3 dc in first corner sp, ch 1, join with hdc in top of beg ch-3. Turn.

Colour key:
= A = C
= B = D

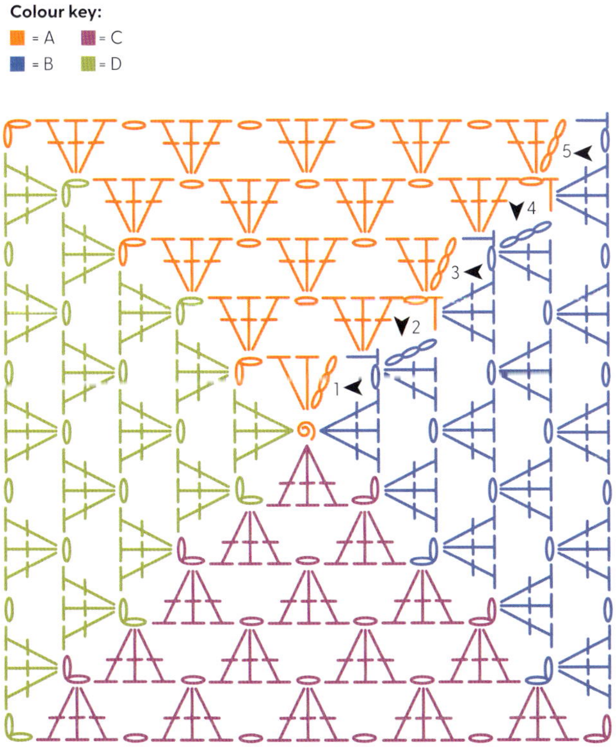

To Modify

* Repeat 4th and 5th rnds to desired size.
* To avoid contrast colour peeking through when working into corner ch-2 sps, use your fingers to slide first 3-dc group in corner up close to same colour stitches beside it.

The Stats

* Worked in join-&-turn rnds
* Requires four colours
* Infinite growth potential
* Reversible
* Pairs well with any square or rectangle, Half Square Triangle 1 or 2

Granny #05

Offset Square

For the non-conformist granny-crocheter, allow me to provide you with a left-(or right)-of-centre option. This granny begins like the Classic Granny, but then switches things up with rows worked along two sides only. Work the rows in a contrast colour to the central square for maximum impact.

Instructions

Make magic ring.

First rnd: Ch 5 (counts as 1 dc, ch-2 sp throughout), [(3 dc, ch 2) 3 times, 2 dc] in ring, join with sl st to 3rd ch of beg ch-5.

2nd rnd: Sl st in first ch-2 sp, ch 5, 3 dc, in same ch-2 sp, ch 1, [(3 dc, ch 2, 3 dc) in next ch-2 sp, ch 1] 3 times, 2 dc in first ch-2 sp, join with sl st to 3rd ch of beg ch-5, sl st in first ch-2 sp. Turn.

From this point forward, square is worked in rows on two sides only.

3rd row: Ch 3 (counts as 1 dc throughout), 1 dc in first dc (counts as 2 dc throughout), ch 1, 3 dc in next ch-1 sp, ch 1, [3 dc, ch 2, 3 dc] in next ch-2 sp, ch 1, 3 dc in next ch-1 sp, ch 1, 2 dc in next ch-2 sp. Turn.

4th row: Ch 3, [3 dc, ch 1] in each ch-1 sp to next ch-2 sp, [3 dc, ch 2, 3 dc] in next ch-2 sp, [ch 1, 3 dc] in each ch-1 sp to end of row, 1 dc in top of ch-3. Turn.

5th row: Ch 3, 1 dc in first dc, ch 1, [3 dc, ch 1] in each ch-1 sp to next ch-2 sp, [3 dc, ch 2, 3 dc] in next ch-2 sp, [ch 1, 3 dc] in each ch-1 sp to end of row, ch 1, 2 dc in top of ch-3. Turn.

If you're particular about it, try working join-&-turn rounds (see The Basics: Turn It Up) before switching to rows for a consistent fabric.

To Modify

* Rep 4th and 5th rows to desired size.
* While these instructions have you switch to rows after just two rnds, you can work a Classic Granny to any size before switching.

The Stats

* Worked in rnds and rows
* Infinite growth potential
* Works best with two colours or more
* Pairs well with Classic Granny, any rectangle, Half Square Triangle 1 or 2

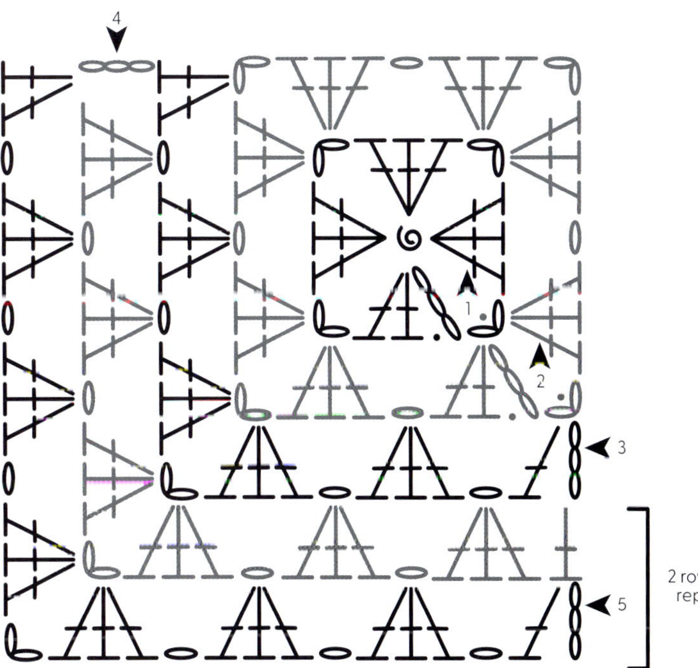

Granny #06

Circle in a Square

It's enormously satisfying to turn a perfectly round shape into a perfect square one with just one round of crochet. This is a really fun motif to play around with colours and create all sorts of spot-on projects.

Instructions

Using A, make magic ring.

First rnd: Using A, ch 4 (counts as 1 dc, ch-1 sp throughout), [3 dc, ch 1] 5 times in ring, 2 dc in ring, join with sl st to 3rd ch of beg ch-4.

2nd rnd: Sl st in first ch-1 sp, ch 4, 2 dc in same ch-1 sp, ch 1, [(2 dc, ch 1) twice in next ch-1 sp] 5 times, 1 dc in first ch-1 sp, join with sl st to 3rd ch of beg ch-4.

3rd rnd: Sl st in first ch-1 sp, ch 4, [3 dc, ch 1] in each ch-1 sp around, 2 dc in first ch-1 sp, join with sl st to 3rd ch of beg ch-4.

4th rnd: Using B, sl st in first ch-1 sp, ch 6 (counts as 1 tr and ch-2 sp), 3 tr in same ch-1 sp, ch 1, (3 dc, ch 1) in each of next 2 ch-1 sps, [(3 tr, ch 2, 3 tr, ch 1) in next ch-1 sp, (3 dc, ch 1) in each of next 2 ch-1 sps] 3 times, 2 tr in first ch-1 sp, join with sl st to 4th ch of beg ch-6.

5th rnd: Sl st in first ch-2 sp, ch 5 (counts as 1 dc and ch-2 sp), 3 dc in same ch-2 sp, ch 1, [(3 dc, ch 1) in each ch-1 sp to next corner ch-2 sp, (3 dc, ch 2, 3 dc) in corner ch-2 sp, ch 1] 3 times, [3 dc, ch 1] in each ch-1 sp to first corner ch-2 sp, 2 dc in first corner ch-2 sp, join with sl st to 3rd ch of beg ch-5.

To Modify

- Rep 5th rnd to desired size.
- Try working all in one shade for a subtle textural pattern.
- To make the circle pop, try working stitches of 4th rnd into back loop only of chains, rather than into ch-1 sps.

The Stats

- Worked in rnds
- Works best with two colours
- Infinite growth potential
- Pairs well with any square or rectangle, Half Square Triangle 1 or 2

Granny #07

Log Cabin Square

Introducing the house that Granny built! The traditional log cabin quilt design translates beautifully to crochet. Piece together several 4-log squares or keep stackin' them logs to infinity for a grand 'ole granny blanket!

Instructions

Base Square: Using A, make Base Square as Classic Granny using join-&-turn rnds, ending on a 4th rnd. Fasten off. Turn.

FIRST LOG

Join B with sl st to any corner ch-2 sp of Base Square. The edge worked across for First Log is top of Log Cabin Square.

First row: Ch 3 (counts as 1 dc throughout), 1 dc in same sp, ch 1, *3 dc in next ch-1 sp, ch 1; rep from * to next corner ch-2 sp, 2 dc in corner ch-2 sp, turn.

2nd row: Ch 3, 3 dc in next ch-1 sp, *ch 1, 3 dc in next ch-1 sp; rep from * to end of row, 1 dc in top of ch-3, turn.

3rd row: Ch 3 (counts as 1 dc throughout), 1 dc in first dc, ch 1, *3 dc in next ch-1 sp, ch 1; rep from * to end of row, 2 dc in top of ch-3, turn.

4th row: As 2nd row, turn. Fasten off.

SECOND LOG

Rotate 90° clockwise. Join C with sl st in top of ch-3 at top-right corner.

First row: Working across left side edge of First Log, ch 3, 1 dc in same sp, ch 1, 3 dc around beg ch-3 from 2nd row of First Log, ch 1, working across left side edge of Base Square, 3 dc in first ch-2 sp, ch 1, *3 dc in next ch-1 sp, ch 1; rep from * to next corner ch-2 sp, 2 dc in corner ch-2 sp, turn.

2nd–4th rows: Work as given for 2nd–4th rows of First Log. Fasten off.

THIRD LOG

Rotate 90° clockwise. Join D with sl st to top of ch-3 at top-right corner.

First row: Working across left side edge of Second Log, ch 3, 1 dc in same sp, ch 1, 3 dc around beg ch-3 from 2nd row of Second Log, ch 1, working across bottom edge of Base Square, 3 dc in first ch-2 sp, ch 1, *3 dc in next ch-1 sp, ch 1; rep from * to next corner ch-2 sp, 2 dc in corner ch-2 sp, turn.

2nd–4th rows: Work as given for 2nd–4th rows of First Log. Fasten off.

FOURTH LOG

Rotate 90° clockwise. Join E with sl st in top of ch-3 at top-right corner.

First row: Working across left side edge of Third Log, ch 3, 1 dc in same sp, ch 1, 3 dc around beg ch-3 from 2nd row of Third Log, ch 1, working across right side edge of Base Square, 3 dc in first ch-2 sp, ch 1, *3 dc in next ch-1 sp, ch 1; rep from * to next corner ch-2 sp, 3 dc in corner ch-2 sp, working across right side edge of First Log, ch 1, 3 dc around last dc from 2nd row of First Log, ch 1, 2 dc in top of last dc of 4th row of First Log, turn.

2nd–4th rows: Work as given for 2nd–4th rows of First Log. Fasten off.

The Stats

- Worked in rnds, then rows
- Infinite growth potential
- Pairs well with any square or rectangle, Half Square Triangle 1 or 2

To Modify

- After Fourth Log is complete work will again be square and basic technique can be repeated, creating more "Logs" around new, larger square.
- Many variations can be created using same log cabin technique by varying size of Base Square, number of rows in each "Log" or beg with a Base Rectangle.

Colour key:

- = Base Square
- = First Log B
- = Second Log C
- = Third Log D
- = Fourth Log E

Granny #08

Tilted Spiral Square

Here's a new twist (groan!) on the traditional granny square! To achieve the spiral effect, two or four colours are used simultaneously in each round, dropping and picking up each colour as needed. I like to draw out and extend the stitch before dropping it to help prevent accidental unravelling. If dropping a "live" stitch still makes you nervous, just slip a stitch marker in 'er before removing that hook.

While you can grow this square to any size, the spiral is less evident the bigger it gets.

Instructions

Notes:

- Work each rnd in the same colour sequence: A, B, C, D.
- When changing colours, leave the colour not in use at the back (WS) of the work.
- Colours in the chart are shown in light and dark versions, alternating each rnd for easier reading.

Using A, make magic ring.

First rnd: Using A, ch 1, [1 sc, 1 hdc, 2 dc] in ring, drop yarn from hook, *join B to ring with sl st after last stitch in A, ch 1, [1 sc, 1 hdc, 2 dc] in ring, drop yarn from hook; rep from * twice more, changing to next colour of sequence with each rep.

2nd rnd: *Pick up A, working across sts in B, 2 dc in first sc, 1 dc in next hdc, 2 dc in next dc, 1 dc in next dc, drop yarn from hook: rep from * three times more, changing to next colour of sequence with each rep.

3rd rnd: *Pick up A, working across sts in B, ch 2, 1 dc in first dc, sk next dc, 2 dc in each of next 2 dc, sk next dc, 1 dc in last dc, drop yarn from hook: rep from * three times more, changing to next colour of sequence with each rep.

4th rnd: *Pick up A, working across sts in B, [2 dc, ch 2, 2 dc] in ch-2 sp, ch 1, [sk next dc, 2 dc in next dc, ch 1] 3 times, drop yarn from hook: rep from * three times more, changing to next colour of sequence with each rep.

5th rnd: *Pick up A, working across sts in B, [3 dc, ch 2, 3 dc] in ch-2 sp, ch 1, sk next 2 dc, [2 dc, ch 1] in each of next 3 ch-1 sps; rep from * three times more, changing to next colour of sequence with each rep.

6th rnd: *Pick up A, working across sts in B, [2 dc, ch 1] in each ch-1 sp to next ch-2 corner sp, [3 dc, ch 2, 3 dc, ch 1] in corner ch-2 sp, [2 dc, ch 1] in each of next 3 ch-1 sps; rep from * three times more, changing to next colour of sequence with each rep.

Note: Final rnd can be worked at this point or after any subsequent rnd.

Final rnd: *Pick up A, working across sts in B, [2 hdc, ch 1] in next ch-1 sp, [2 sc, ch 1] in next ch-1 sp, sl st in next ch-1 sp, fasten off; rep from * three times more, changing to next colour of sequence with each rep.

The Stats

- Requires two or four colours
- Infinite growth potential
- Pairs well with any square or rectangle, Half Square Triangles 1 or 2

To Modify

- Repeat 6th rnd to desired size then complete with Final rnd.
- To work in two shades simply alternate A and B shades, replacing references to C with A and D with B.

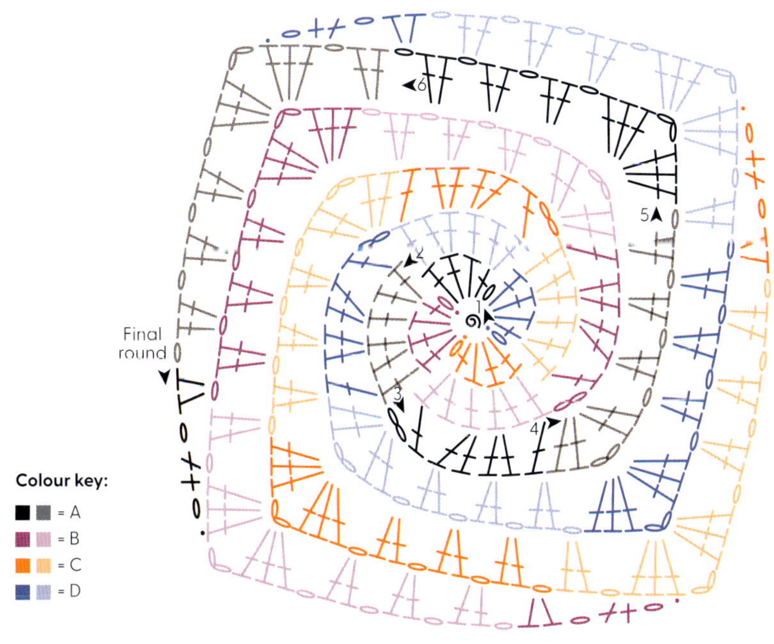

Granny #09

Mitred Square

Mitre? I hardly know her! This square, which is worked diagonally corner-to-corner, can yield really interesting patchwork combinations when the stripes and orientation are varied. So knock granny off her axis and see what you think!

Instructions

Make magic ring.

First row (RS): Ch 3, (counts as 1 dc throughout), [1 dc, ch 2, 2 dc] in ring. Turn.

2nd row: Ch 3, [3 dc, ch 2, 3 dc] in next ch-2 sp, 1 dc in top of ch-3. Turn.

3rd row: Ch 3, 1 dc in first dc (counts as 2 dc throughout), ch 1, [3 dc, ch 2, 3 dc] in next ch-2 sp, ch 1, 2 dc in top of ch-3. Turn.

4th row: Ch 3, [3 dc, ch 1] in each ch-1 sp to next ch-2 sp, [3 dc, ch 2, 3 dc] in next ch-2 sp, [ch-1, 3 dc] in each ch-1 sp to end of row, 1 dc in top of ch-3. Turn.

5th row: Ch 3, 1 dc in first dc, ch 1, [3 dc, ch-1] in each ch-1 sp to next ch-2 sp, [3 dc, ch 2, 3 dc] in next ch-2 sp, [ch 1, 3 dc] in each ch-1 sp to end of row, ch 1, 2 dc in top of ch-3. Turn.

To Modify

* Repeat 4th and 5th rows to desired size.
* If changing colours each row, you can choose to work with right side facing at all times: simply fasten off at end of row, ditch turn, then join new yarn with a sl st to first st of last row. Follow all other instructions as given.

The Stats

* Worked in rows
* Infinite growth potential
* Pairs well with Granny Stitch in Rows, Half Square Triangle 1 or 2, any rectangle

Try combining the Mitred Square with her cousin the Mitred Corner Rectangle!

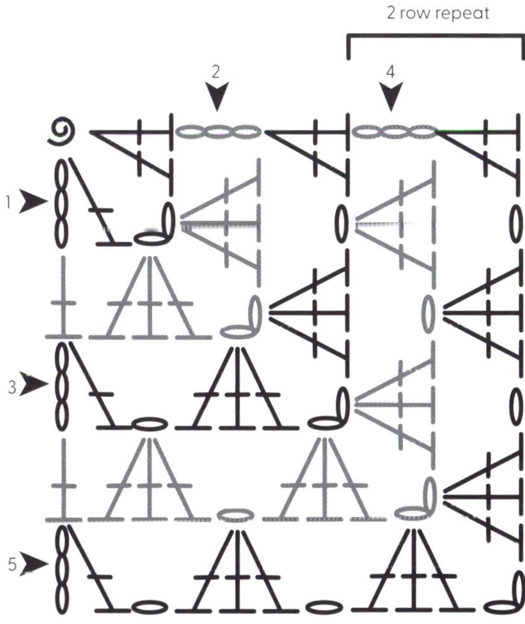

Granny #10

Diamond in a Square

A fun and easy way to level-up your granny! Four triangles are worked onto the sides of a base square and voila - a dynamic twist on a classic. As an added bonus, once you've completed one diamond-in-a-square, you can keep building on it creating an infinite diamond-in-a-square-in-a-diamond-in-a-square... you get the picture. Work the base square in a contrasting colour to the triangles for maximum impact!

Instructions

This shape is worked in both rounds and rows, so use join-&-turn rounds as indicated for a consistent fabric.

Base Square: Make a Base Square using instructions for Classic Granny in join-&-turn rnds, ending on 4th rnd, 10, 16, 22 rnd or any rnd in increments of six thereafter. Fasten off.

First Triangle: With preferred RS facing, join yarn with sl st to centre dc of 3-dcCL directly to right of centre ch-1 sp at any side edge of Base Square.

First row: Ch 1, [3 dc, ch 2, 3 dc] in centre ch-1 sp of Base Square, ch 1, sk next dc, sl st in next dc, ch 4 (counts as 1 dc, ch-1 sp throughout), sk next dc and ch-1 sp, sl st in next dc. Turn.

2nd row: Sl st in first 2 ch of ch-4, working across prev Triangle row, 2 dc in first ch-1 sp, ch 1, [3 dc, ch 2, 3 dc] in next ch-2 sp, ch 1, 3 dc in last ch-1 sp, ch 1, working across last rnd of Base Square, sk first unworked dc and next ch 1 sp, sl st in next dc, ch 4 (counts as 1 dc, ch-1 sp), sk next 2 dc, sl st in next ch sp. Turn.

3rd row: Sl st in first 2 ch of ch-4, working across prev Triangle row, 2 dc in first ch-1 sp, ch 1, [3 dc, ch 1] in each ch-1 sp to next ch-2 sp, [3 dc, ch 2, 3 dc] in next ch-2 sp, ch 1, [3 dc, ch 1] in each ch-1 sp to end of row, ch 1, working across last rnd of Base Square, sk next 2 unworked sts, sl st in next st **, ch 4 (counts as 1 dc, ch-1 sp), sk next 2 sts, sl st in next st of Base Square. Turn.

Rep 3rd row until last row ends at Base Square corner ch-2 sp, ending last rep of 3rd row at **. Fasten off.

2nd to 4th Triangles: Make as for First Triangle, working across each side of Base Square, beg with same side facing each time.

To Modify

- To keep building new Diamonds-in-Squares, first add plain rnds to ensure you have right number of 3-dcCL at each side to work Triangles.

With preferred RS facing, join yarn with sl st to corner ch-2 sp of any Triangle.

First rnd: Ch 5 (counts as 1 dc, ch-2 sp throughout), 3 dc in same ch-2 sp, ch 1, [3 dc, ch 1] in each ch-1 sp to centre sp where triangles meet, 3 dc in ch-2 corner sp of base square, ch 1, [3 dc, ch 1] in each ch-1 sp to next corner ch-2 sp, *[3 dc, ch 2, 3 dc]in corner ch-2 sp, ch 1, [3 dc, ch 1] in each ch-1 sp to centre sp where triangles meet, 3 dc in ch-2 corner sp of base square, ch 1, [3 dc, ch 1] in each ch-1 sp to next corner ch-2 sp; rep from * around, 2 dc in first corner ch-2 sp, join with sl st to 3rd ch of beg ch-5. Turn.

Rnds 2–4: Sl st in first ch-2 sp, ch 5, 3 dc in same ch-2 sp, ch 1, [(3 dc, ch 1) in each ch-1 sp to next corner ch-2 sp, (3 dc, ch 2, 3 dc) in corner ch-2 sp, ch 1] 3 times, [3 dc, ch 1] in each ch-1 sp to first corner ch-2 sp, 2 dc in first corner ch-2 sp, join with sl st to 3rd ch of beg ch-5, turn.

After 4th rnd begin adding Triangles, treating this as new Base Square.

The Stats

- Worked in rnds and then rows
- Infinite growth potential
- Pairs well with Classic Granny, Half Square Triangle 1 or 2, any rectangle

Colour key:

- = Base Square A
- = Triangle B
- = Plain rounds/ New Base Square C

Chart shows square with extra rounds, ready to add more triangles

Granny #11

Acute Triangle

Wanna make a-cute triangle (groan!)? This nice and narrow shape is worked from the bottom point upwards towards a straight edge, and grows in width equally on both sides to create the shape.

Instructions

Ch 4.

First row: 2 dc in 4th ch from hook (skipped ch-3 counts as 1 dc). Turn.

2nd row: Ch 3 (counts as 1 dc throughout), 1 dc in first dc, ch 1, sk next dc, 1 dc in top of ch-4. Turn.

3rd row: Ch 4 (counts as 1 dc, ch-1 sp throughout), 3 dc in next ch-1 sp, ch 1, 1 dc in top of ch-3. Turn.

4th row: Ch 3, 3 dc in first ch-1 sp, ch 1, 3 dc in next ch-1 sp, 1 dc in 3rd ch of ch-4. Turn.

5th row: Ch 3, 2 dc in first dc, ch 1, 3 dc in next ch-1 sp, ch 1, 3 dc in top of ch-3. Turn.

6th row: Ch 3, 1 dc in first dc, ch 1, [3 dc, ch 1] in each ch-1 sp to last 3 sts, 2 dc in top of ch-3. Turn.

7th row: Ch 4, [3 dc, ch 1] in each ch-1 sp to last 2 sts, 1 dc in top of ch-3. Turn.

8th row: Ch 3, 3 dc in first ch-1 sp, [ch 1, 3 dc] in each ch-1 sp to last st, 1 dc in 3rd ch of ch-4. Turn.

9th row: Ch 3, 2 dc in first dc, ch 1, [3 dc, ch 1] in each ch-1 sp to last 4 sts, 3 dc in top of ch-3. Turn.

The Stats

- Worked in rows, tip-out
- Infinite growth potential
- Reversible
- Pairs well with itself

To Modify

- Rep 6th–9th rows to desired size.

Equilateral Triangle

If geometry isn't your jam, allow me to point out that the equilateral triangle is one in which all sides are equal (if only this were true in life!). This triangle doesn't play as nicely with squares as the Half Square Triangle, but all things created equal, it doesn't have to. A batch of equilateral triangles on their own can create a lot of very interesting designs.

Instructions

Make magic ring.

First rnd: Ch 7 (counts as 1 dc, ch-4 throughout), [4 dc, ch 4] twice in ring, 3 dc in ring, join with sl st to 3rd ch of beg ch-7.

2nd rnd: Sl st in first 2 ch, ch 7, 4 dc in same ch-4 sp, ch 2, [(4 dc, ch 4, 4 dc, ch 2) in next ch-4 sp] twice, 3 dc in first ch-4 sp, join with sl st to 3rd ch of beg ch-7.

3rd rnd: Sl st in first 2 ch, ch 7, 4 dc in same ch-4 sp, ch 2, 4 dc in next ch-2 sp, ch 2, *[4 dc, ch 4, 4 dc, ch 2] in next ch-4 sp, 4 dc in next ch-2 sp, ch 2; rep from * around, 3 dc in first ch-4 sp, join with sl st to 3rd ch of beg ch-7.

4th rnd: Sl st in first 2 ch, ch 7, 4 dc in same ch-4 sp, ch 2, [4 dc in next ch-2 sp, ch 2] to next corner ch-4 sp, *[4 dc, ch 4, 4 dc] in next corner ch-4 sp, ch 2, [4 dc in next ch-2 sp, ch 2] to next corner ch-4 sp; rep from * around, 3 dc in first ch-4 sp, join with sl st to 3rd ch of beg ch-7.

To Modify

- Rep 4th rnd to desired dimensions.

The Stats

- Worked in rnds
- Infinite growth potential
- Pairs well with itself and Hexagon

Combine six equilateral triangles to form a hexagon!

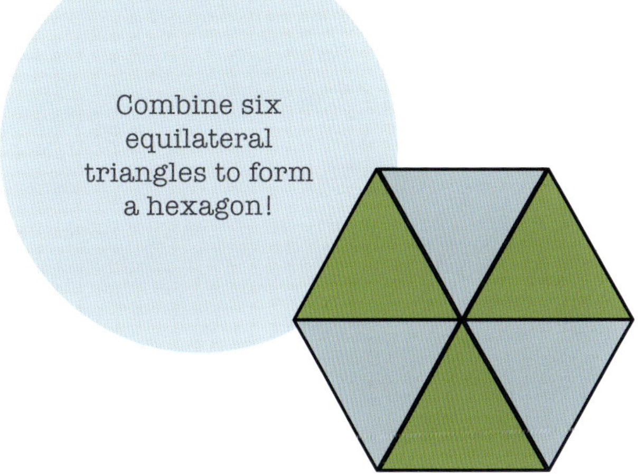

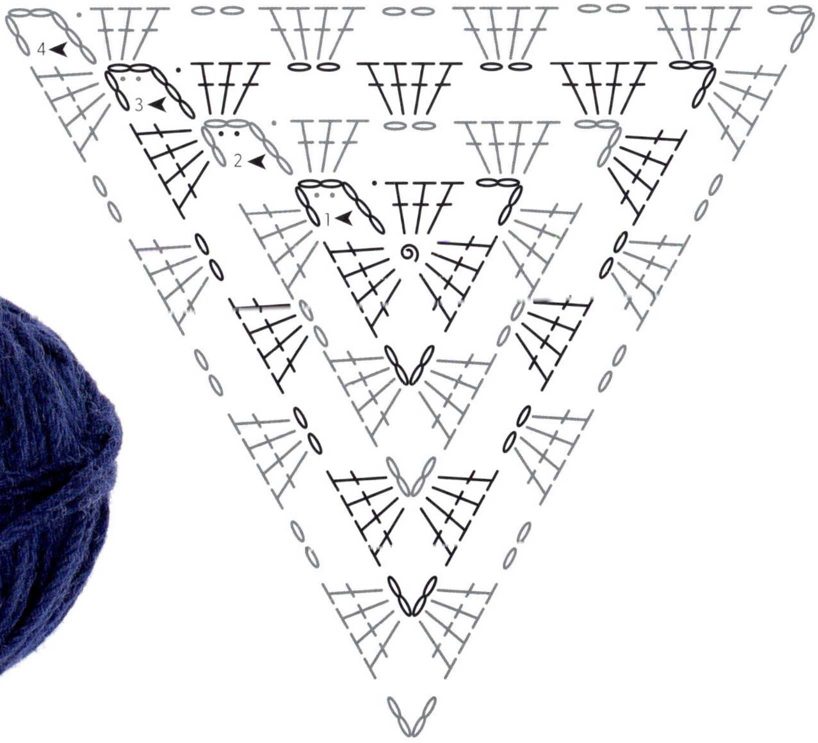

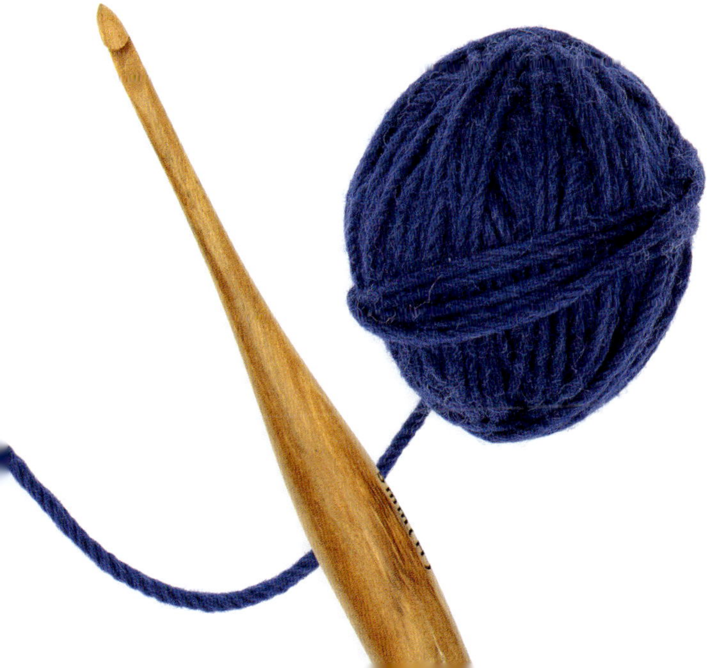

Granny #13

Half Diamond Triangle 1

This is essentially an equilateral triangle, though worked from one side up instead of from the centre-out. Use it with the Diamond and the Half Diamond Triangle 2 for diamond-studded patchwork projects with squared-off edges.

Instructions

Make magic ring.

First row: Ch 3 (counts as 1 dc throughout), [4 dc, ch 4, 5 dc] in ring. Turn.

2nd row: Ch 3, 3 dc in first dc, ch 2, [4 dc, ch4, 4 dc] in ch-4 sp, ch 2, 4 dc in top of ch-3. Turn.

3rd row: Ch 3, 1 dc in first dc, ch 2, 4 dc in next ch-2 sp, ch 2, [4 dc, ch 4, 4 dc] in next ch-4 sp, ch 2, 4 dc in next ch-2 sp, ch 2, 2 dc in top of ch-3. Turn.

4th row: Ch 4 (counts as 1 dc, ch-1 sp), [4 dc, ch 2] in each ch-2 sp to next ch-4 sp, [4 dc, ch 4, 4 dc] in next ch-4 sp], [ch 2, 4 dc] in each ch-2 sp to last 2 sts, ch 1, 1 dc in top of ch-3. Turn.

5th row: Ch 3, 3 dc in first ch-1 sp, ch 2, [4 dc, ch 2] in each ch-2 sp to next ch-4 sp, [4 dc, ch 4, 4 dc] in next ch-4 sp, ch 2, [4 dc, ch 2] in each ch-2 sp to last ch-4 sp, 3 dc in last ch-1 sp, 1 dc in 3rd ch of ch-4. Turn.

6th row: Ch 3, 1 dc in first dc, ch 2, [4 dc, ch 2] in each ch-2 sp to next ch-4 sp, [4 dc, ch 4, 4 dc] in next ch-4 sp, ch 2, [4 dc, ch 2] in each ch-2 sp to last 4 sts, 2 dc in top of ch-3. Turn.

To Modify

* Rep 4th–6th rows to desired size.

The Stats

* Worked in rows
* Infinite growth potential
* Pairs well with Half Diamond Triangle 2, Diamond

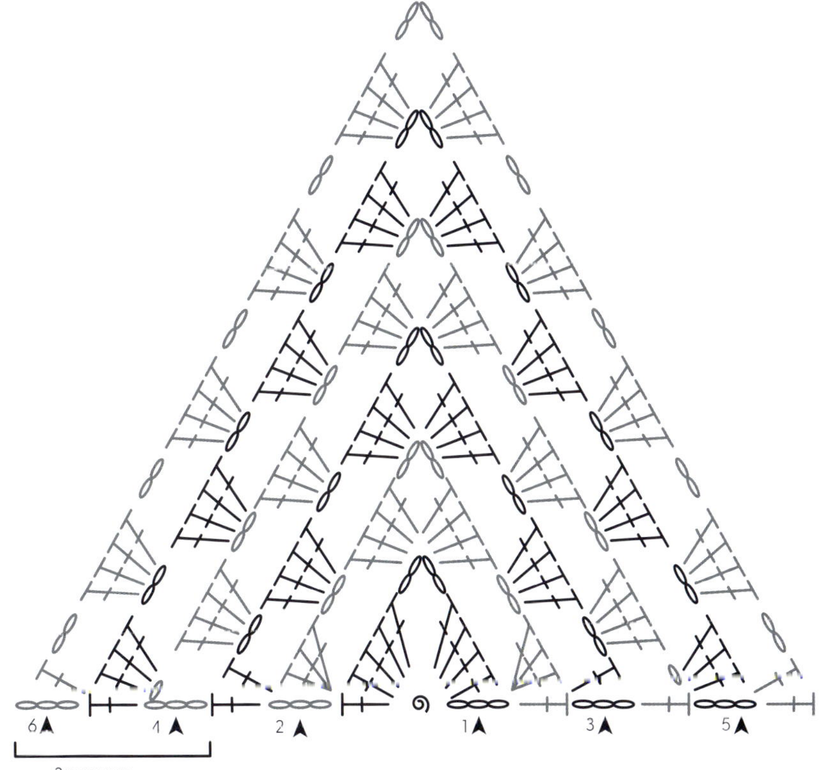

Granny #14

Half Diamond Triangle 2

This wide triangle fits perfectly with the Diamond and the Half Diamond Triangle 1 to use for patchwork projects. Used on its own, the proportions are also great for a shawl.

Try finishing with a round of single crochet (see The Finishing: Living on the Edge) for clean edges.

Instructions

Make magic ring.

First row: Ch 5 (counts as 1 tr, ch-1 sp throughout), [4 dc, ch 2, 4 dc, ch 1, 1 tr] in ring. Turn.

2nd row: Ch 5, 4 dc in first ch-1 sp, ch 2, [3 dc, ch 2, 3 dc] in next ch-2 sp, ch 2, 4 dc in next ch-1 sp, ch 1, 1 tr in 4th ch of ch-5. Turn.

3rd row: Ch 5, 4 dc in first ch-1 sp, ch 2, 4 dc in next ch-2 sp, ch 2, [1 dc, ch 2 (corner), 1 dc] in next ch-2 sp, ch 2, 4 dc in next ch-2 sp, ch 2, 4 dc in next ch-1 sp, ch 1, 1 tr in 4th ch of ch-5. Turn.

4th row: Ch 5, 4 dc in first ch-1 sp, [ch 2, 4 dc] in each ch-2 sp to corner ch-2 sp, ch 4, sk corner ch-2 sp, [4 dc, ch 2] in each ch-2 sp to last ch-1 sp, 4 dc in last ch-1 sp, ch 1, 1 tr in 4th ch of ch-5. Turn.

5th row: Ch 5, 4 dc in first ch-1 sp, ch 2, [4 dc, ch-2] in each ch-2 sp to next ch-4 sp, [3 dc, ch 2 (corner), 3 dc] in next ch-4 sp, [ch 2, 4 dc] in each ch-2 sp to last ch-1 sp, ch 2, 4 dc in last ch-1 sp, ch 1, 1 tr in 4th ch of ch-5. Turn.

6th row: Ch 5, 4 dc in first ch-1 sp, ch 2, [4 dc, ch 2] in each ch-2 sp to corner ch-2 sp, [1 dc, ch 2 (corner), 1 dc] in corner ch-2 sp, [ch 2, 4 dc] in each ch-2 sp to last ch-1 sp, ch 2, 4 dc in last ch-1 sp, ch 1, 1 tr in 4th ch of ch-5. Turn.

To Modify

* Rep 4th–6th rows to desired size.

The Stats

* Worked in rows
* Infinite growth potential
* Pairs well with Diamond, Half Diamond Triangle 1

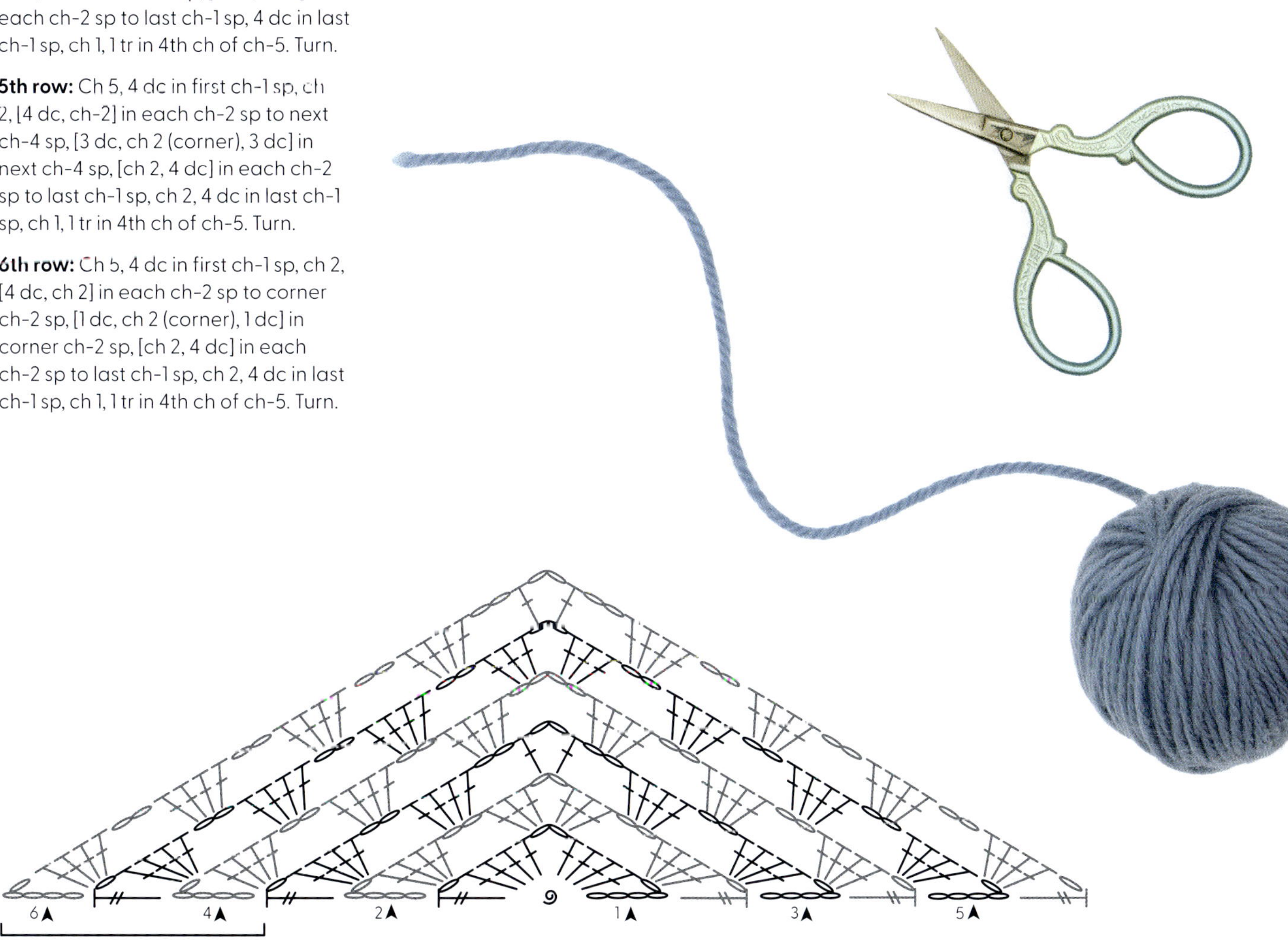

Granny #15

Half Square Triangle 1

This is a handy little shape to have around. Combined with the Classic Granny you can create easy simple shaping for garments. It's also a great fill-in shape, straightening out the sides of projects made with octagons, parallelograms or squares (when placed at 45 degrees). Of course, used solely on its own: this triangle has still got the right (angled) stuff.

Instructions

Make magic ring.

First row (RS): Ch 5 (counts as 1 dc, ch-2 sp throughout), [3 dc, ch 2, 3 dc, ch 2, 1 dc] in ring. Turn.

2nd row (WS): Ch 5, 3 dc in first ch-2 sp, ch 1, [3 dc, ch 2, 3 dc] in next ch-2 sp, ch 1, 3 dc in last ch-2 sp, ch 2, 1 dc in 3rd ch of ch-5. Turn.

3rd row: Ch 5, 3 dc in first ch-2 sp, ch 1, 3 dc in next ch-1 sp, ch 1, [3 dc, ch 2, 3 dc] in next ch-2 sp, ch 1, 3 dc in next ch-1 sp, ch 1, 3 dc in last ch-2 sp, ch 2, 1 dc in 3rd ch of ch-5. Turn.

4th row: Ch 5, 3 dc in first ch-2 sp, ch 1, [3 dc in next ch-1 sp, ch 1] to next ch-2 sp, [3 dc, ch 2, 3 dc] in next ch-2 sp, ch 1, [3 dc in next ch-1 sp, ch 1] to last ch-2 sp, 3 dc in last ch-2 sp, ch 2, 1 dc in 3rd ch of ch-5. Turn.

To Modify

- Rep 4th row to desired size.
- If you find long edge of triangle (where rows begin and end) has too much fabric, reduce chain at beg of each row to ch-4 and end each row with "ch-1, 3 dc in 3rd ch of beg ch-4".

The Stats

- Infinite growth potential
- Worked in rows
- Pairs well with any square, Octagon, Parallelogram

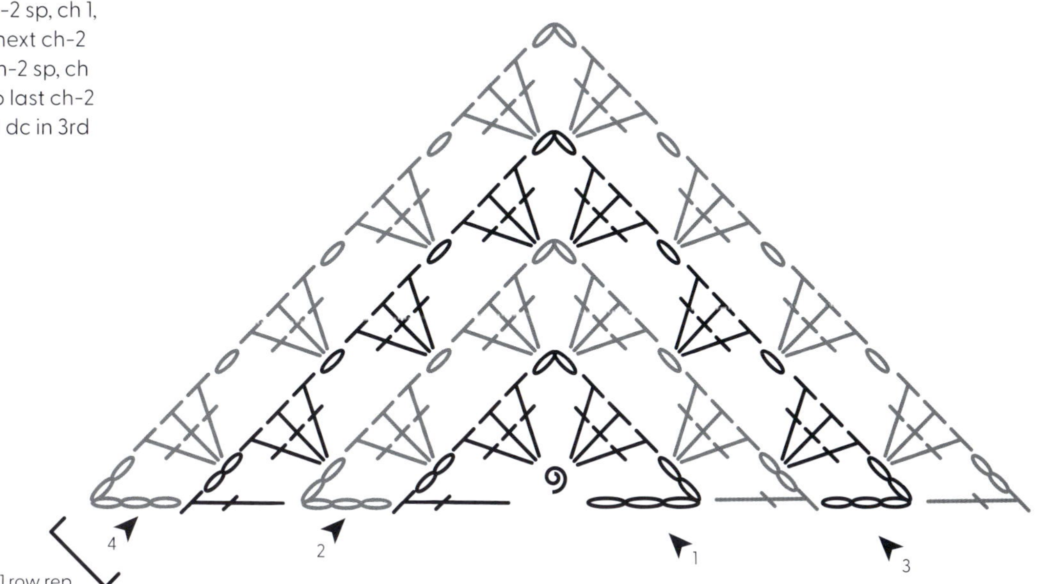

Granny #16

Half Square Triangle 2

The Half Square Triangle 1 and 2 have the same proportions, but these two are definitely fraternal twins. While #1 is essentially a Classic Granny cut in half diagonally, this guy begins at one corner and each row is worked straight across. The differences between the two are more pronounced when worked in stripes: Version 1 would have L-shaped stripes, while Version 2 here has straight stripes across the shape.

Instructions

Ch 4.

First row: 2 dc in 4th ch from hook (skipped ch-3 counts as 1 dc). Turn.

2nd row: Ch 3 (counts as 1 dc throughout), 3 dc in first dc, sk next dc, 1 dc in last dc. Turn.

3rd row : Ch 3, 1 dc in first dc, ch 1, sk next 3 dc, 4 dc in top of ch-3. Turn.

4th row: Ch 3, 3 dc in first dc, ch 1, sk next 3 dc, 3 dc in next ch-1 sp, sk next dc, 1 dc in last dc. Turn.

5th row: Ch 3, 1 dc in first dc, ch 1, 3 dc in next ch-1 sp, ch 1, 4 dc in top of ch-3. Turn.

6th row: Ch 3, 3 dc in first dc, [ch 1, 3 dc] in each ch-1 sp to last 2 sts, 1 dc in top of ch-3. Turn.

7th row: Ch 3, 1 dc in first dc, ch 1, [3 dc, ch 1] in each ch-1 sp to last 4 sts, 4 dc in top of ch-3. Turn.

To Modify

- Rep 6th and 7th rows to desired size.
- To be a true-blue half-square, width of last row should be equal to height of all rows. Because stitch height can vary from person to person, proportions of this version may not always be exactly equal to half a square.

The Stats

- Worked in rows
- Reversible
- Infinite growth potential
- Pairs well with any square or rectangle, Half Square Triangle 1

Granny #17

Half Rectangle Triangle

This triangle, along with the Half Square Triangle belongs to the right-angled family. This sister-from-another-mister (Mr Right?) is twice as tall as she is wide at any size. It's the perfect shape to frame the edges of a diamond to create a rectangle.

Instructions

Ch 4.

First row: 2 dc in 4th ch from hook (skipped ch-3 counts as 1 dc). Turn.

2nd row: Ch 3 (counts as 1 dc throughout), 2 dc in first dc, sk next dc, 1 dc in top of ch-3. Turn.

3rd row: Ch 3, 1 dc in first dc, ch 1, sk next 2 dc, 2 dc in top of ch-3. Turn.

4th row: Ch 4 (counts as 1 dc and ch-1 sp throughout), 3 dc in next ch-1 sp, 1 dc in top of ch-3. Turn.

5th row: Ch 3, 1 dc in first dc, ch 1, 3 dc in next ch-1 sp, 1 dc in top of ch-3. Turn.

6th row: Ch 3, 2 dc in first dc, [ch 1, 3 dc] in each ch-1 sp to last 2 sts, 1 dc in top of ch-3. Turn.

7th row: Ch 3, 1 dc in first dc, ch 1, [3 dc, ch 1] in each ch-1 sp to last 3 sts, 2 dc in top of ch-3. Turn.

8th row: Ch 4, 3 dc in first ch-1 sp, [ch 1, 3 dc] in each ch-1 sp to last 2 sts, 1 dc in top of ch-3. Turn.

9th row: Ch 3, 1 dc in first dc, [ch 1, 3 dc] in each ch-1 sp to last st, 1 dc in 3rd ch of ch-4.

To Modify

- Rep Rows 6-9 to desired size.
- The right angle will fall on the right as written, but simply flip the shape to have it on the left.

The Stats

- Worked in rows
- Reversible
- Infinite growth potential
- Pairs well with the Diamond, and any square or rectangle

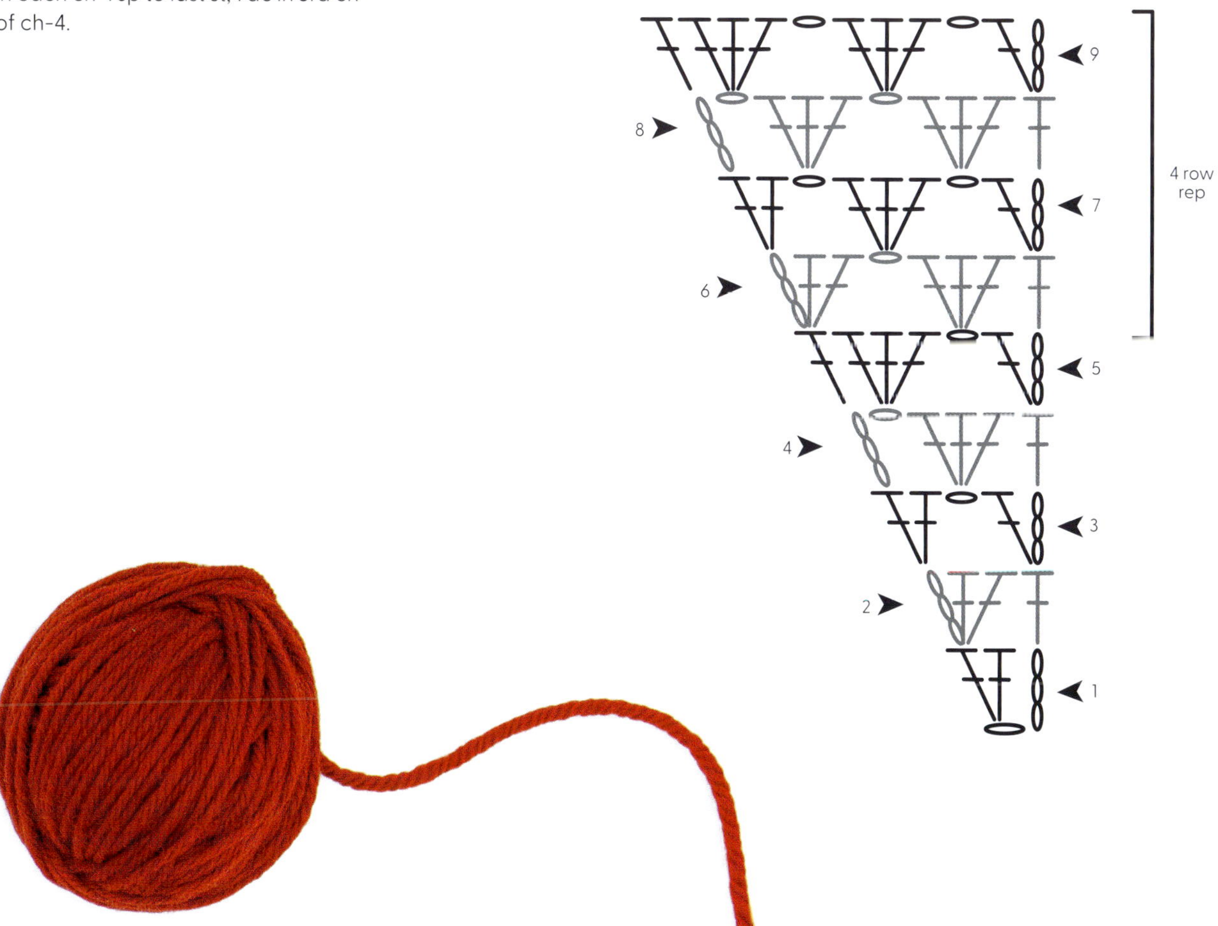

Granny #18

Obtuse Triangle

Obtuse, but not difficult, this is my go-to granny pattern for making a simple triangular shawl. Beginning at the tip, this triangle has an easy-to-memorize one-row repeat that makes for wonderfully mindless crocheting.

Instructions

Ch 4.

First row: 2 dc in 4th ch from hook (skipped ch-3 counts as 1 dc). Turn.

2nd row: Ch 3 (counts as 1 dc throughout), 2 dc in first dc, ch 1, sk next dc, 3 dc in top of ch-3. Turn.

3rd row: Ch 3, 2 dc in first dc, ch 1, 3 dc in next ch-1 sp, ch 1, 3 dc in top of ch-3. Turn.

4th row: Ch 3, 2 dc in first dc, ch 1, [3 dc, ch 1] in each ch-1 sp to last 3 dc, 3 dc in top of ch-3. Turn.

To Modify

* Rep 4th row to desired size.

The Stats

* Worked in rows
* Infinite growth potential
* Pairs well with itself

This pattern makes a great no-waste shawl as the tip-out construction means you can just keep crocheting until you run out of yarn!

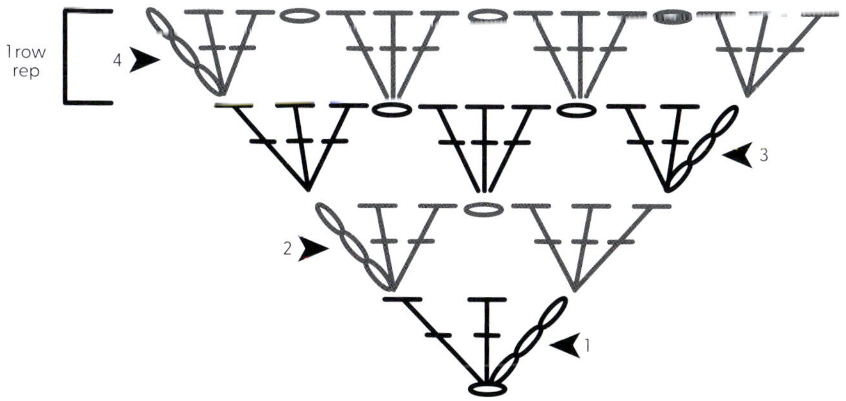

1 row rep
4
3
2
1

Granny #19

Simple Circle

This pattern yields nice, well-rounded results (pun very much intended) at any size. It's great all on its own for coasters, placemats, blankets or whatever circle you want to run in!

Circle not laying flat? Try working one more or one less "plain" 3-dc cluster round between the increase rounds.

Instructions

Work between 2nd and 3rd dc when working into 4-dcCL.

Make magic ring.

First rnd: Ch 4 (counts as 1 dc, ch-1 sp throughout), [2 dc, ch 1] 5 times in ring, 1 dc in ring, join with sl st to 3rd ch of beg ch-4.

2nd rnd: Sl st in first ch-1 sp, ch 4, [4 dc, ch 1] in each ch-1 sp around, 3 dc in first ch-1 sp, join with sl st to 3rd ch of beg ch-4.

3rd rnd: Sl st in first ch-1 sp, ch 4, *3 dc in next 4-dcCL, ch 1, 3 dc in next ch-1 sp, ch 1, rep from * to last 4-dcCL, 3 dc in last 4-dcCL, ch 1, 2 dc in first ch-1 sp, join with sl st to 3rd ch of beg ch-4.

4th rnd: Sl st in first ch-1 sp, ch 4, [4 dc, ch 1] in each ch-1 sp around, 3 dc in first ch-1 sp, join with sl st to 3rd ch of beg ch-4.

5th rnd: Sl st in first ch-1 sp, ch 4, *2 dc in next 4-dcCL, ch 1, 2 dc in next ch-1 sp, ch 1, rep from * to last 4-dcCL, 2 dc in last 4-dcCL, ch 1, 1 dc in first ch-1 sp, join with sl st to 3rd ch of beg ch-4.

6th rnd: Sl st in first ch-1 sp, ch 4, [3 dc, ch 1] in each ch-1 sp around, 2 dc in first ch-1 sp, join with sl st to 3rd ch of beg ch-4.

7th rnd: Sl st in first ch-1 sp, ch 4, 3 dc in next ch-1 sp, ch 1, *4 dc in next ch-1 sp, ch 1, 3 dc in next ch-1 sp, ch 1; rep from * to last ch-1 sp, 3 dc in last ch-1 sp, join with sl st to 3rd ch of beg ch-4.

8th rnd: Sl st in first ch-1 sp, ch 4, 2 dc in next ch-1 sp, ch 1, 2 dc in next 4-dcCL, ch 1, *[2 dc, ch 1] in each of next 2 ch-1 sps, 2 dc in next 4-dcCL, ch 1; rep from * around, 1 dc in first ch-1 sp, join with sl st to 3rd ch of beg ch-4.

9th and 10th rnds: As 6th rnd.

11th rnd: As 7th rnd, working 1 additional [3 dc, ch 1] between each 4-dcCL.

12th rnd: As 8th rnd, working [2 dc, ch-1] in each ch-1 sp and between 2nd and 3rd dc of each 4-dcCL around.

13th rnd: As 6th rnd.

To Modify

- To enlarge Simple Circle and shapes based on a circle, let your stitches do the talking rather than following a strict pattern of repeated rounds. So essentially, follow general pattern already established:

1. Work "plain" rounds (those using only 3-dcCLs) until work begins to curl up slightly at edges. This tells you to add sts. Number of plain rounds may be same as prev or one or two more depending on individual gauge and stitch height.
2. Increase with evenly-spaced 4-dcCLs as in prev round using 4-dcCLs, but add one additional 3-dcCL between 4-dcCLs.
3. Work a round with 2-dcCLs as prev, working into centre of 4-dcCLs.
4. Rep Steps 1–3 as many times as you like!

The Stats

- Worked in rnds
- Infinite growth potential
- Does not pair well with much, to be honest. This shape likes to roll on its own!

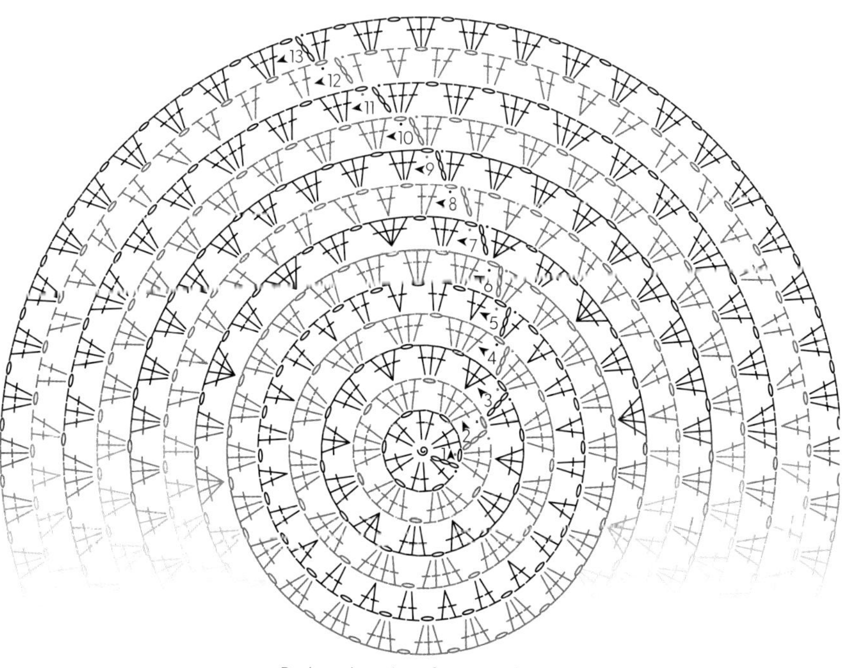

Reduced section of pattern shown

Granny #20

Half Circle

A half circle is twice as flexible as a whole one when it comes to combining with other shapes. That nice, flat side can buddy up with almost any straight-sided shape! In a fine yarn this would make a great shawl, or try it in jumbo yarn for a sweet semi-circle rug.

Instructions

Make magic ring.

First row: Ch 4 (counts 1 dc and ch 1 sp throughout), [2 dc, ch 1] twice in ring, 1 dc in ring. Turn.

2nd row: Ch 3 (counts as 1 dc throughout), 3 dc in first ch-1 sp, ch 1, 4 dc in next ch 1 sp, ch 1, 3 dc in last ch-1 sp, 1 dc in 3rd ch of ch-4. Turn.

3rd row: Ch 3, 3 dc between first and 2nd dc of first 3-dcCL, ch 1, 3 dc in next ch-1 sp, ch 1, 3 dc between 2nd and 3rd dc of next 4-dcCL, ch 1, 3 dc in next ch-1 sp, ch 1, 3 dc between 2nd and 3rd dc of last 3-dcCL, 1 dc in top of ch-3. Turn.

4th row: Ch 3, 2 dc in first dc, ch 1, [4 dc, ch 1] in each ch-1 sp to end of row, 3 dc in top of ch-3. Turn.

5th row: Ch 3, 1 dc in first dc, ch 1, 2 dc in next ch-1 sp, *ch 1, 2 dc between 2nd and 3rd dc of next 4-dcCL, ch 1, 2 dc in next ch-1 sp; rep from * to end of row, ch 1, 2 dc in top of ch-3. Turn.

6th row: Ch 4, [3 dc, ch 1] in each ch-1 sp to end of row, 1 dc in top of ch-3. Turn.

7th row: Ch 3, 2 dc in first ch-1 sp, ch 1, 4 dc in next ch-1 sp, ch 1, *3 dc in next ch 1 sp, ch 1, 4 dc in next ch-1 sp, ch 1; rep from * to last ch-4 sp, 2 dc in last ch-4 sp, 1 dc in 3rd ch of ch-4. Turn.

8th row: Ch 3, 1 dc in first dc, ch 1, *2 dc in next ch-1 sp, ch 1, 2 dc between 2nd and 3rd dc of next 4-dcCL, ch 1, 2 dc in next ch 1 sp, ch-1; rep from * to end of row, 2 dc in top of ch-3. Turn.

9th row: Rep 6th row.

10th row: Ch 3, 2 dc in first ch-1 sp, ch 1, [3 dc, ch 1] in each ch-1 sp to last ch-4 sp, 2 dc in last ch-4 sp, 1 dc in ch-3, 3rd ch of ch-4. Turn.

11th row: Ch 4, 4 dc in next ch-1 sp, ch 1, *[3 dc in next ch-1 sp, ch 1] twice, 4 dc in next ch-1 sp, ch 1; rep from * to end of row, 1 dc in top of ch-3. Turn.

12th row: As 8th row, working 2-dcCLs into each ch-1 sp and between 2nd and 3rd dc of each 4-dcCL.

13th row: Rep 6th row.

The Stats

- Worked in rows
- Infinite growth potential
- Pairs well with Classic Granny, any rectangle, Pentagon

To Modify

- To enlarge Half Circle, see To Modify: Simple Circle. Note that how you begin and end each row is dependent on the stitches of the previous row and may take some trial and error to maintain a straight edge.
- Wanna add some Half Circles directly to side of Classic Granny or other straight-sided shape? Check out instructions in Heart.

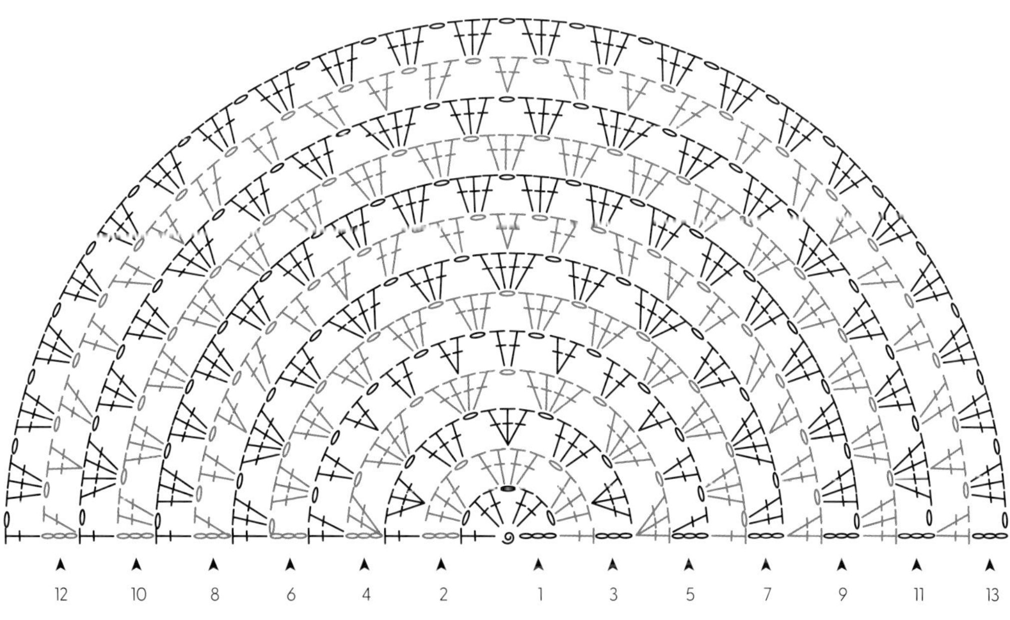

Granny #21

Quarter Circle

This sassy little segment is quite handy for taking the edge off (corner edges, that is). Try replacing the corner squares in a granny square blanket with a quarter circle and you've got yourself a sweet rounded-edge finish.

Instructions

Note: Work between 2nd and 3rd dc when working into cluster.

Make magic ring.

First row: Ch 3 (counts as 1 dc throughout), 4 dc in ring. Turn.

2nd row: Ch 3, 2 dc in first dc, ch 1, sk next 3 dc, 3 dc in top of ch-3. Turn.

3rd row: Ch 3, 2 dc in first dc, ch 1, 3 dc in next ch-1 sp, ch 1, 3 dc in top of ch-3. Turn.

4th row: Ch 4 (counts as 1 dc, ch-1 sp throughout), [4 dc, ch 1] in each of next 2 ch-2 sps, 1 dc in top of ch-3.

5th row: Ch 3, [2 dc in next ch-1 sp, ch 1, 2 dc in next 4-dcCL, ch 1] twice, 2 dc in next ch-1 sp, 1 dc in top of ch-3. Turn.

6th row: Ch 3, 1 dc in first dc, ch 1, [3 dc, ch 1] in each ch-1 sp to end of row, 2 dc in top of ch-3. Turn.

7th row: Ch 3, [4 dc in next ch-1 sp, ch 1, 3 dc in next ch-1 sp, ch 1] twice, 4 dc in next ch-1 sp, 1 dc in top of ch-3. Turn.

8th row: Ch 3, 1 dc in first dc, ch 1, 2 dc in next 4-dcCL, ch 1, *[2 dc in next ch-1 sp, ch 1] twice, 2 dc in next 4-dcCL, ch 1; rep from * to last st, 1 dc in top of ch-3. Turn.

9th row: Ch 4, [3 dc, ch 1] in each ch-1 sp to end of row, 1 dc in top of ch-3. Turn.

10th row: Ch 3, 2 dc in first ch-1 sp, ch 1, [3 dc, ch 1] in each ch-1 sp to last ch-4 sp, 2 dc in last ch-4 sp, 1 dc in 3rd ch of ch-4. Turn.

11th row: Ch 4, 4 dc in next ch-1 sp, ch 1, *[3 dc, ch 1] in each of next 2 ch-1 sps, 4 dc in next ch-1 sp, ch 1; rep from * to last ch-1 sp, [3 dc, ch 1] in last ch-1 sp, 1 dc in top of ch-3. Turn.

12th row: Ch 3, 2 dc in first ch-1 sp, ch 1, 2 dc in next ch-1 sp, ch 1, 2 dc in next 4-dcCL, ch 1, *[2 dc in next ch-1 sp, ch 1] 3 times, 2 dc in next 4-dcCL, ch 1; rep from * to last ch-4 sp, ch 1, 2 dc in ch-4 sp, 1 dc 3rd ch of ch-4. Turn.

13th row: Rep 9th row.

To Modify

- Row repeat for increasing Quarter Circle works best if you let your crochet do the talking rather than following a strict formula. As personal st height and gauge of each crocheter varies, number of plain rows you need to work between increases to maintain straight edges will vary, too. Row rep will look something like this:

  Next X rows: Rep 10th row, then 9th row until work begins to slightly pull inward.

  Next row: As 11th row, working one additional 3-dcCL between each 4-dcCL.

  Next row: As 12th row, working 2-dcCLs into each ch-1 sp and between 2nd and 3rd dc of each 4-dcCL.

The Stats

- Worked in rows
- Infinite growth potential
- Pairs well any square or rectangle

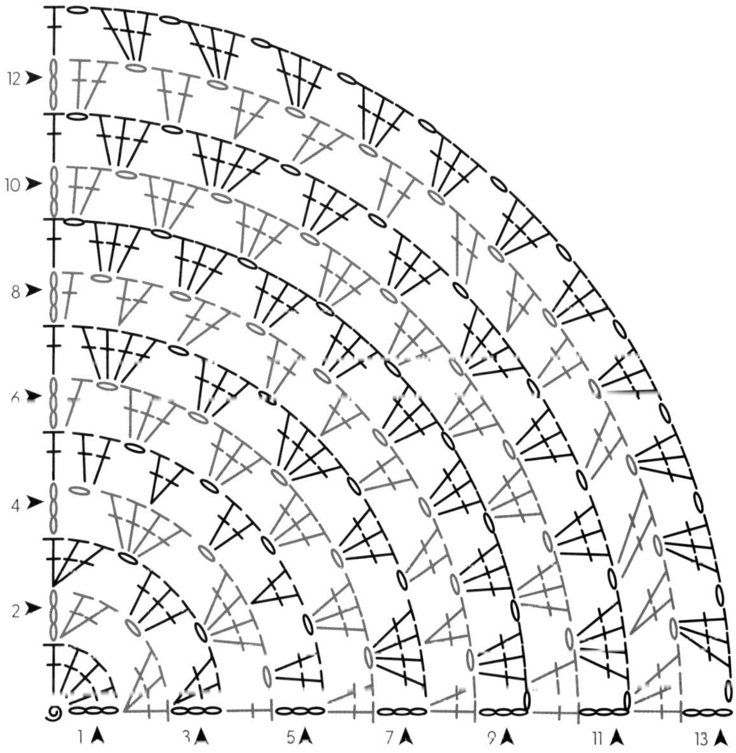

Flower

This shape is my homage to Orla Kiely, the fashion designer famous for her graphic, botanical prints. Equally cute at three or four rounds and easily J.A.Y.go-ed together, this granny's got a lot of flower power!

Instructions

Using A, make magic ring.

First rnd: Ch 3 (counts as 1 dc), 15 dc in ring, join with sl st in top of beg ch-3.

2nd rnd: Sl st in sp between first two dc, ch 4 (counts as 1 dc, ch-1), *sk next 2 dc, 3 dc between last skipped dc and next dc, ch 1; rep from * to last 2 sts, 2 dc in same sp as first sl st, join with sl st to 3rd ch of beg ch-4. Break A.

3rd rnd: Join B with sl st to any ch-1 sp, *ch 1, sk next 3 dc, [2 dc, ch 1] 4 times in next ch-1 sp, sk next 3 dc, sl st in next ch-1 sp; rep from * around.

4th rnd: *Ch 2, sk next ch-1 sp, [4 dc in next ch-1 sp, ch 1] twice, 4 dc in next ch-1 sp, ch 2, sk next ch-1 sp, sl st in next ch-1 sp of 2nd rnd; rep from * around.

Fasten off.

To Modify

- Stop after three rnds for teenier blossom.
- To J.A.Y.go multiple flowers together, join flowers together during 3rd or 4th rnd with sl sts in ch-1 sps (indicated in red on chart).

  To join during 3rd rnd: Replace first and 3rd ch-1 sps of each petal with sl st to adjacent Flower.

  To join during 4th rnd: Replace each ch-1 sps with sl st to adjacent Flower.
- Four-petal construction means this flower is almost square and can be patched together quite well with square motifs.

The Stats

- Worked in rnds
- Works best with two colours
- Ideal for J.A.Y.go seaming
- Pairs well with Classic Granny, Leaf

Granny #23

Oval

Granny placemats, anyone? A granny rug? The oval (or perhaps more accurately, the rounded rectangle) might just be the shape you never knew you needed. Beginning with an adjustable foundation chain, you can re-size this opulent oval to your heart's content.

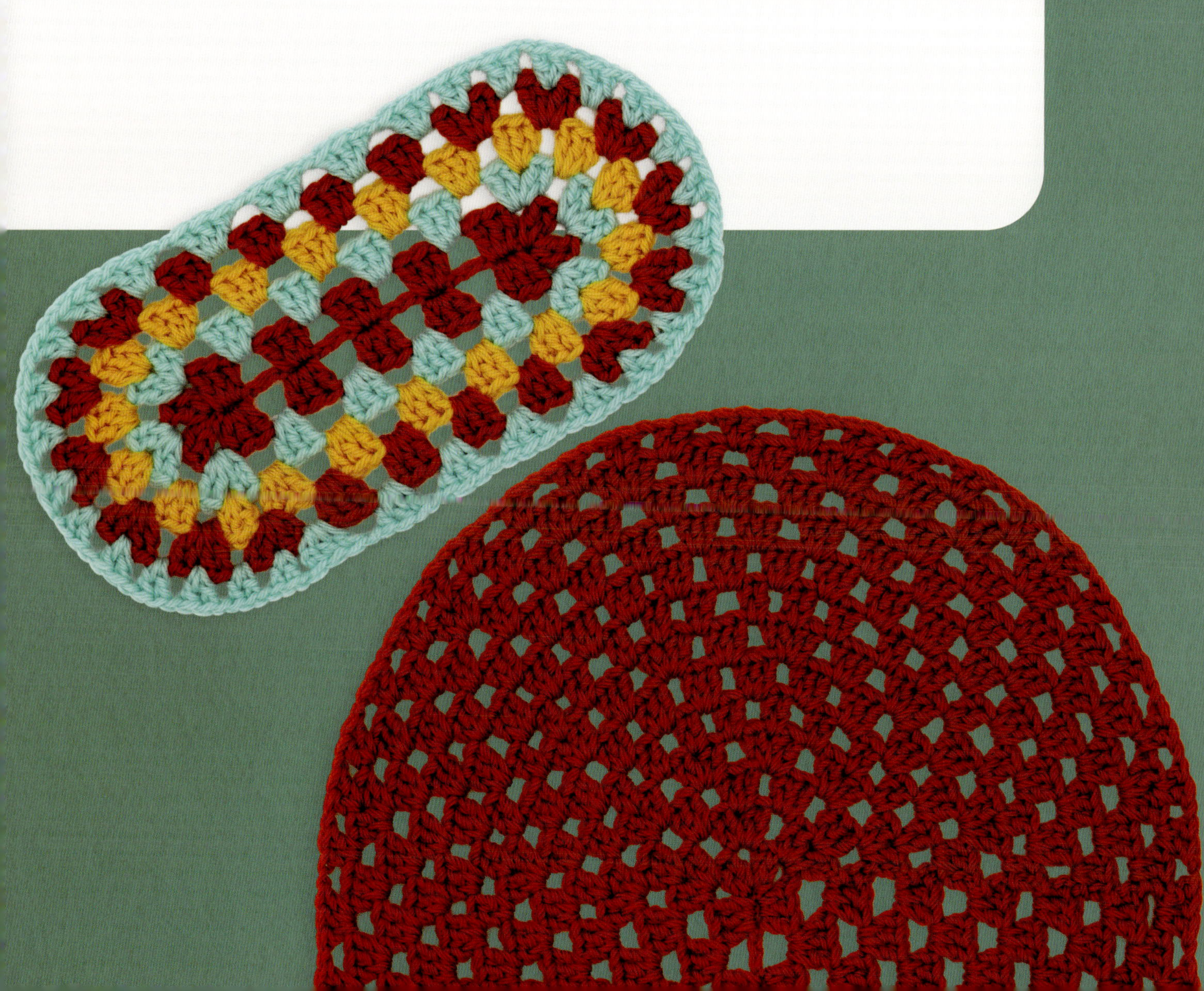

Instructions

Note: Work between 2nd and 3rd dc when working into cluster.

Ch 15 (multiple of 4 plus 3, min. of 15).

First rnd: 3 dc in 6th ch from hook (skipped ch-5 counts as 1 dc, ch-1 sp, sk 1 ch), [ch 1, sk next 3 ch, 3 dc in next ch] twice, [ch 1, 2 dc] twice in last ch, working across opposite side of foundation chain, ch 1, 3 dc in next ch, [ch 1, sk next 3 ch, 3 dc in next ch] twice, [ch 1, 2 dc, ch 1, 1 dc] in next ch, join with sl st to 4th ch of beg ch-5.

2nd rnd: Sl st in first ch-1 sp, ch 4 (counts as 1 dc, ch-1 sp throughout), [3 dc in next ch-1 sp, ch 1] twice, [4 dc in next ch-1 sp, ch 1] 3 times, [3 dc in next ch-1 sp, ch 1] twice, [4 dc in next ch-1 sp, ch 1] twice, 3 dc in first ch-1 sp, join with sl st to 3rd ch of beg ch-4.

3rd rnd: Sl st in first ch-1 sp, ch 3 (counts as 1 dc throughout), 2 dc in same sp, [ch 1, 3 dc in next ch-1 sp] twice, [ch 1, 3 dc in next 4-dcCL, ch 1, 3 dc in next ch-1 sp] 3 times, [ch 1, 3 dc in next ch-1 sp] twice, [ch 1, 3 dc in next 4-dcCL, ch 1, 3 dc in next ch-1 sp] twice, ch 1, 3 dc in next 3-dcCL, ch 1, join with sl st in top of beg ch-3.

4th rnd: Ch 4, [3 dc in next ch-1 sp, ch 1] twice, [4 dc in next ch-1 sp, ch 1] 6 times, [3 dc in next ch-1 sp, ch 1] twice, [4 dc in next ch-1 sp, ch 1] 5 times, 3 dc in last ch-1 sp, join with sl st to 3rd ch of beg ch-4.

5th rnd: Sl st in first ch-1 sp, ch 3, 2 dc in same sp, ch 1, [3 dc in next ch-1 sp, ch 1] twice, [2 dc in next 4-dcCL, ch 1, 2 dc in next ch-1 sp, ch 1] 5 times, 2 dc in next 4-dcCL, [ch 1, 3 dc in next ch-1 sp] 3 times, ch 1, [2 dc in next 4-dcCL, ch 1, 2 dc in next ch-1 sp, ch 1] 5 times, 2 dc in next 3-dcCL, ch 1, join with sl st in top of beg ch-3.

6th rnd: Ch 4, [3 dc, ch 1] in each ch-1 sp to last ch-1 sp, 2 dc in last ch-1 sp, join with sl st to 3rd ch of beg ch-4.

7th rnd: Sl st in first ch-1 sp, ch 3, 2 dc in same sp, ch 1, [3 dc in next ch-1 sp, ch 1] twice, [4 dc in next ch-1 sp, ch 1, 3 dc in next ch-1 sp, ch 1] 6 times, [3 dc in next ch-1 sp, ch 1] twice, [4 dc in next ch-1 sp, ch 1, 3 dc in next ch-1 sp, ch 1] 5 times, 4 dc in next ch-1 sp, ch 1, join with sl st in top of beg ch-3.

8th rnd: Ch 4, [3 dc in next ch-1 sp, ch 1] twice, [2 dc in next ch-1 sp, ch 1, 2 dc in next 4-dcCL, ch 1, 2 dc in next ch-1 sp, ch 1] 6 times, [3 dc in next ch-1 sp, ch 1] twice, [2 dc in next ch-1 sp, ch 1, 2 dc in next 4-dcCL, ch 1, 2 dc in next ch-1 sp, ch 1] 5times, 2 dc in next ch-1 sp, ch 1, 2 dc in next 4-dcCL, ch 1, 1 dc in last ch-1 sp, join with sl st to 3rd ch of beg ch-4.

9th rnd: Sl st in first ch-1 sp, ch 3, 2 dc in same sp, ch 1, [3 dc in next ch-1 sp, ch 1] around. Join with sl st in top of beg ch-3.

10th rnd: Rep 6th rnd.

11th rnd: Rep 9th rnd.

12th rnd: Ch 4, [3 dc in next ch-1 sp, ch 1] 3 times, [4 dc in next ch-1 sp, ch 1, (3 dc in next ch-1 sp, ch 1) twice] 6 times, [3 dc in next ch-1 sp, ch 1] twice, [4 dc in next ch-1 sp, ch 1, (3 dc in next ch-1 sp, ch 1) twice] 5 times, 4 dc in next ch-1 sp, ch 1, 2 dc in last ch-1 sp, join with sl st to 3rd ch of beg ch-4.

13th rnd: Sl st in first ch-1 sp, ch 3, 2 dc in same sp, ch 1, [3 dc in next ch-1 sp, ch 1] twice, 2 dc in next ch-1 sp, ch 1, *[2 dc in next 4-dcCL, ch 1, (2 dc in next ch-1 sp, ch 1) 3 times] 5 times, 2 dc in next 4-dcCL, ch 1, 2 dc in next ch-1 sp, ch 1 **, [3 dc in next ch-1 sp, ch 1] 3 times, 2 dc in next ch-1 sp, ch 1, rep from * to ** once more, join with sl st in top of beg ch-3.

To Modify

- To add rounds, see To Modify: Simple Circle. Note that you will need to maintain straight sides of shape by only working increases at rounded ends of Oval.
- Oval can be lengthened by adding multiples of 4 chains to the foundation chain.

The Stats

- Worked in rnds
- Adjustable length and width

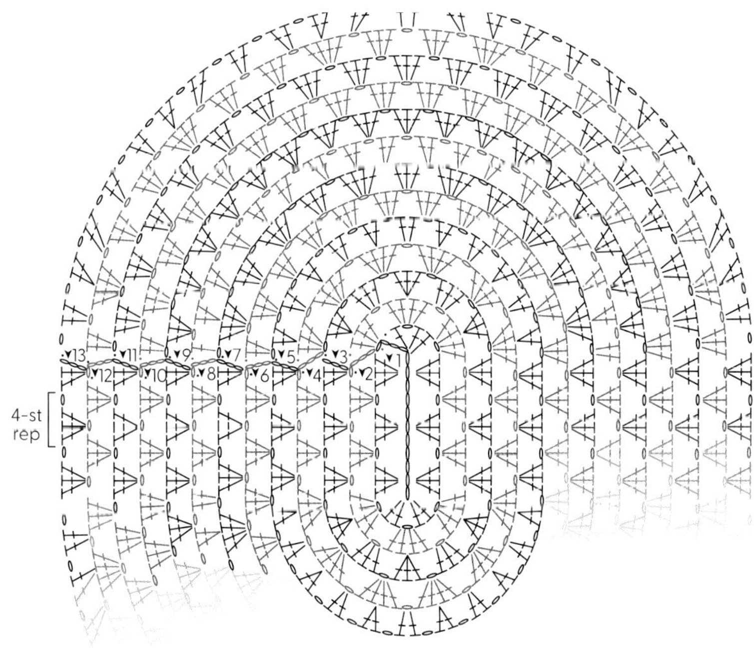

Reduced section of pattern shown

Granny #24

Egg

Egg? Avocado? This shape starts with two circular rounds, which you can work in a contrasting colour for a "yoke" or "pit" if you so desire. But even made in just one solid shade, this ovoid is truly eggs-ellent.

Instructions

Work between 2nd and 3rd st when working into cluster.

Make magic ring.

First rnd: Ch 4 (counts 1 dc, ch-1 sp throughout), [2 dc, ch 1] 5 times in ring, 1 dc in ring, join with sl st to 3rd ch of beg ch-4.

2nd rnd: Sl st in first ch-1 sp, ch 4, [4 dc, ch 1] in each ch-1 sp around, 3 dc in first ch-1 sp, join with sl st to 3rd ch of beg ch-4.

3rd rnd: Sl st in first ch-1 sp, ch 4, [3 dc in next 4-dcCL, ch 1, 3 dc in next ch-1 sp, ch 1] 3 times, 3 dc in next 4-dcCL, ch 1, 3 tr in next ch-1 sp, ch 1, 4 tr in next 4-dcCL, ch 1, 3 tr in in next ch-1 sp, ch 1, 3 dc in next 4-dcCL, ch 1, 2 dc in first ch-1 sp, join with sl st to 3rd ch of beg ch-4.

4th rnd: Sl st in first ch-1 sp, ch 4, [4 dc in next ch-1 sp, ch 1] 7 times, 4 tr in next ch-1 sp, ch 1, 4 tr in next 4-trCL, ch 1, 4 tr in next ch-1 sp, ch-1 [4 dc in next ch-1 sp, ch 1] twice, 3 dc in first ch-1 sp, join with sl st to 3rd ch of beg ch-4.

5th rnd: Sl st in first ch-1 sp, ch 4, [2 dc in next 4-dcCL, ch 1, 2 dc in next ch-1 sp, ch 1] 7 times, 2 tr in next 4-trCL, ch 1, 2 tr in next ch-1 sp, [ch 1, 2 tr, ch 1, 2 tr] in next 4-trCL, ch 1, 2 tr in next ch-1 sp, ch 1, 2 tr in next 4-trCL, ch 1, [2 dc in next ch-1 sp, ch 1, 2 dc in next 4-dcCL, ch 1] 3 times, 1 dc in first ch-1 sp, join with sl st to 3rd ch of beg ch-4.

Fasten off.

To Modify

- Work first 3 or 4 rnds only for smaller egg.

The Stats

- Worked in rnds
- Shape established at 3rd rnd
- Pairs well with Toast! (Just kidding, this shape doesn't pair easily)

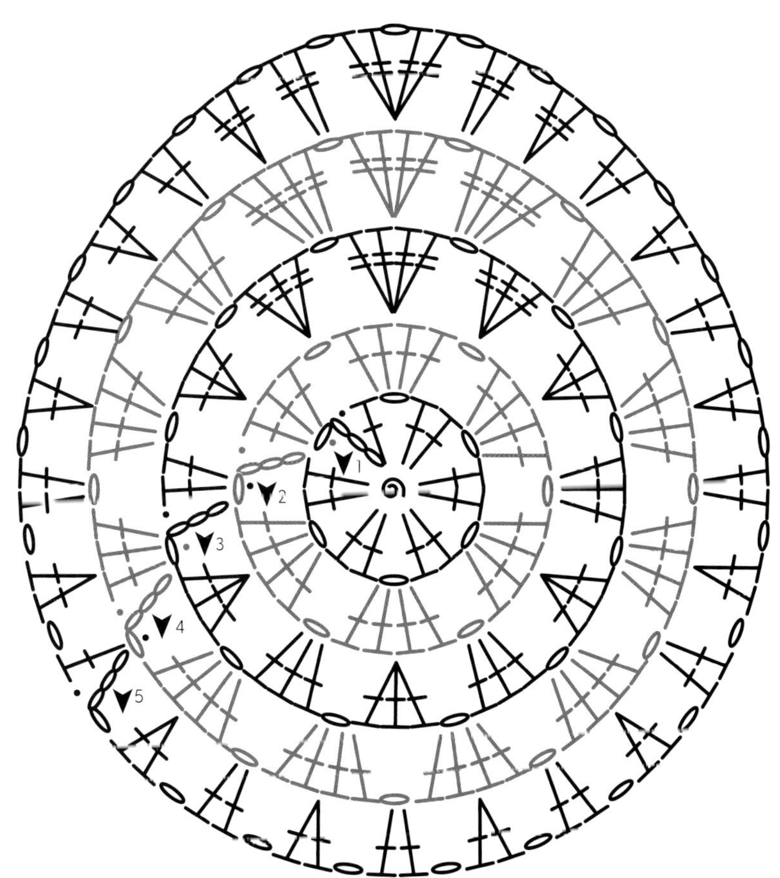

Granny #25

Heart

This design (much like myself) is a square at heart. Easily adaptable to different sizes, this love-ly shape begins with a Classic Granny, then gets a-round with a couple of half circles. Go kick start your granny heart!

Instructions

Base Square: Make Base Square as Classic Granny using join-&-turn rnds, ending on a 4th rnd. Fasten off. Turn.

First Half Circle: Locate centre ch-1 sp at any side of Base Square. Join yarn with sl st to centre dc of 3-dcCL directly to right of centre ch-1 sp.

First row: Ch 1, [2 dc, ch 1] twice in centre ch-1 sp of Base Square, sk next dc, sl st in each of next 2 dc and next ch-1 sp. Turn.

2nd row: Working across prev Half Circle row, 3 dc in first ch-1 sp, ch 1, 4 dc in next ch-1 sp, ch 1, 3 dc in next ch-1 sp, working across last rnd of Base Square, sk first unworked dc, sl st in next ch-1 sp and next 2 dc. Turn.

3rd row: Working across prev Half Circle row, ch 1, 3 dc between first and 2nd dc of next 3-dcCL, ch 1, [3 dc in next ch-1 sp, ch 1, 3 dc between 2nd and 3rd dc of next CL, ch 1] twice, working across last rnd of Base Square, sk first unworked dc, sl st in next 2 dc and corner ch-2 sp. Turn.

4th row: Working across prev Half Circle row, 2 dc in first ch-1 sp, ch 1, [4 dc, ch 1] in each of next 4 ch-1 sps, 2 dc in last ch-1 sp, working across last rnd of Base Square, sk first unworked dc, sl st in corner ch-2 sp.

Fasten off.

2nd Half Circle: Make as given for First Half Circle, joining yarn to adjacent side of Base Square.

To Modify

- If changing colours, fasten off at the end of each Half Circle row after the first sl st join to the Base Square. Join the new colour for your next row with a sl st in the space indicated for the last sl st of the previous row.
- To enlarge Heart (without high blood pressure), first work larger Base Square with even number of rnds. Work 1st–4th rnds of First Half Circle, then, continuing same pattern of sl sts to join rows to Base Square, follow 5th row and beyond from Half Circle, eliminating first and last sts of each row until Half Circle meets corners of Base Square.
- Any version of Classic Granny will work for Base Square though using join-&-turn rnds, which have both RS and WS rows, will create most consistent looking fabric when you switch to working in rows for Half Circles.
- For a nice, clean edge, try adding Single Crochet Border around Heart (see The Finishing: Living On The Edge).

The Stats

- Worked in rnds and then rows
- Infinite growth potential
- Pairs well with Classic Granny, Half Square Triangle 1 or 2, any rectangle

Colour key:

= Base Square (Classic Granny worked in join-&-turn rounds)

= Half Circle

Granny #26

Arch

The only thing you'll find at the end of this rainbow is a fasten off. Of course, should you want to crochet a pot of gold, I highly recommend the Half Circle for your pot and the Simple Circle for some gold coins.

Instructions

Note: Work between 2nd and 3rd dc when working into cluster.

Ch 46 (multiple of 8 plus 6, minimum of 30).

First row: 3 dc in 7th ch from hook (skipped ch-6 counts as 1 dc, ch 1, sk 2), [ch 1, sk next 3 ch, 3 dc in next ch] 3 times, [ch 1, sk next 2 ch, 3 dc in next ch] 4 times, [ch 1, sk next 3 ch, 3 dc in next ch] 3 times, ch 1, sk next 2 ch, 1 dc in last ch. Turn.

2nd row: Ch 3 (counts as 1 dc throughout), 2 dc in first ch-1 sp, [ch 1, 3 dc in next ch-1 sp] 3 times, [ch 1, 4 dc in next ch-1 sp] 4 times, [ch 1, 3 dc in next ch-1 sp] 3 times, ch 1, 2 dc in last ch-1 sp, 1 dc in 2nd ch of skipped ch-6. Turn.

3rd row: Ch 4 (counts as 1 dc, ch-1 sp throughout), [3 dc in next ch-1 sp, ch 1] 3 times, [2 dc in next ch-1 sp, ch 1, 2 dc in next 4-dcCL, ch 1] 4 times, 2 dc in next ch-1 sp, ch 1, [3 dc in next ch-1 sp, ch 1] 3 times, 1 dc in top of ch-3. Turn.

4th row: Ch 3, 2 dc in first ch-1 sp, ch 1, *3 dc in next ch-1 sp, ch 1; rep from * to last ch-1 sp, 2 dc in last ch-1 sp, 1 dc in 3rd ch of ch-4. Turn.

5th row: Ch 4, [3 dc in next ch-1 sp, ch 1] twice, [4 dc in next ch-1 sp, ch 1, 3 dc in next ch-1 sp, ch 1] 6 times, 3 dc in next ch-1 sp, ch 1, 1 dc in top of ch-3. Turn.

6th row: Ch 3, 2 dc in first ch-1 sp, [ch 1, 3 dc in next ch-1 sp] twice, [ch 1, 2 dc in next 4-dcCL, ch 1, 2 dc in each of next 2 ch-1 sps] 5 times, ch 1, 2 dc in next 4-dcCL, ch 1, [3 dc in next ch-1 sp, ch 1] twice, ch 1, 2 dc in last ch-1 sp, 1 dc in top of ch-3. Turn.

7th row: Ch 4, *3 dc in next ch-1 sp, ch 1; rep from * to last 3 dc, ch 1, 1 dc in top of ch-3. Turn.

8th row: As 4th row.

9th row: Ch 4, [3 dc in next ch-1 sp, ch 1] 4 times, [4 dc in next ch-1 sp, ch 1, (3 dc, ch 1) in each of next 2 ch-1 sps] 5 times, [3 dc in next ch-1 sp, ch 1] twice, 1 dc in top of ch-3. Turn.

10th row: Ch 3, 2 dc in first ch-1 sp, [ch 1, 3 dc in next ch-1 sp] 3 times, ch 1, 2 dc in next ch-1 sp, ch 1, [2 dc in next 4-dcCL, ch 1, (2 dc, ch 1) in each of next 3 ch-1 sps] 4 times, 2 dc in next 4-dcCL, ch 1, 2 dc in next ch-1 sp, ch 1, [3 dc in next ch-1 sp, ch 1] 3 times, 2 dc in last ch-1 sp, 1 dc top of ch-3. Turn.

11th row: As 7th row.

12th row: As 4th row.

To Modify

- Height of Arch can be modified by adding or subtracting multiples of 8 to foundation chain. Each 8 ch added will require you to add one additional [ch 1, sk next 3 ch, 3 dc in next ch] at beg and end of first row.
- Row rep to enlarge Arch works best if you let your crochet do the talking rather than following a strict formula. To continue to grow Arch beyond 11th row, rep 7th and 8th rows until work begins to cup slightly around Arch. Then increase by repeating 9th row, adding one more 3-dcCL between each 4-dcCL on each rep of increase row. From there, rep 10th row, working 2-dcCLs around Arch and beg and ending each row with three 3-dcCLs. Finally, rep 7th and 8th rows until you need to increase again.

The Stats

- Worked in rows
- Infinite growth potential
- Reversible
- Pairs well with Classic Granny, any rectangle, Single Crochet Border

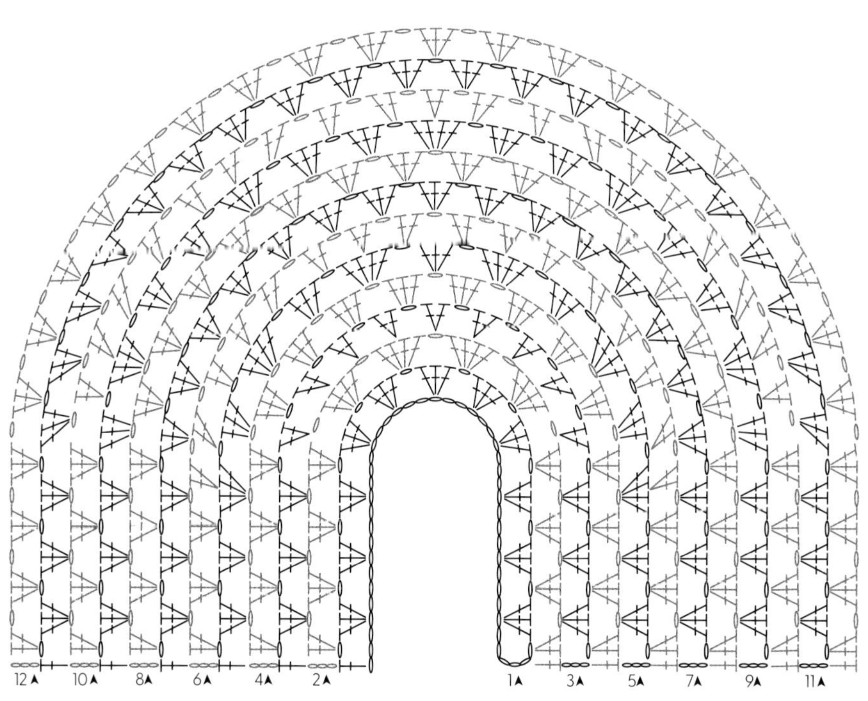

Granny #27

Tulip*

I love a graphic floral pattern and what flower is more graphic than a tulip? The height and width of this budding blossom are equal, meaning it works together nicely with squares for unconventional patchwork projects.

Use the Tulip, the Leaf and the Flower in combination for beauteous botanical appliqués!

Instructions

Note: Work between 2nd and 3rd dc when working into cluster.

Make magic ring.

First row: Ch 3 (counts as 1 dc throughout), [2 dc, ch 1] 3 times in ring, 3 dc in ring. Turn.

2nd row: Ch 3, 2 dc in first dc, ch 1, [4 dc in next ch-1 sp, ch 1] 3 times, 3 dc in top of ch-3. Turn.

3rd row: Ch 3, 2 dc in first dc, ch 1, 3 dc in next ch-1 sp, ch 1, [3 dc in next 4-dcCL, ch 1, 3 dc in next ch-1 sp, ch 1] 3 times, 3 dc in top of ch-3. Turn.

4th row: Ch 3, 2 dc in first dc, ch 1, 3 dc in first ch-1 sp, ch 1, [4 dc in next ch-1 sp, ch 1] 6 times, 3 dc in next ch-1 sp, ch 1, 3 dc in top of ch-3. Turn.

5th row: Ch 3, 2 dc in first dc, ch 1, [3 dc in next ch-1 sp, ch-1] twice, [2 dc in next 4-dcCL, ch 1, 2 dc in next ch-1 sp, ch 1] 5 times, 2 dc in next 4-dcCL, ch 1, [3 dc in next ch-1 sp, ch 1] twice, 3 dc in top of ch-3. Turn.

6th row: Ch 3, 2 dc in first dc, ch 1, [3 dc, ch 1] in each ch-1 sp to end of row, 3 dc in top of ch-3.

Fasten off.

To Modify

* As Tulip shape is established in first row, work any number of fewer rows for a smaller Tulip.

The Stats

* Worked in rows
* Shape established after first row
* Reversible
* Pairs well with any square, Half Square Triangle 1 or 2, Leaf

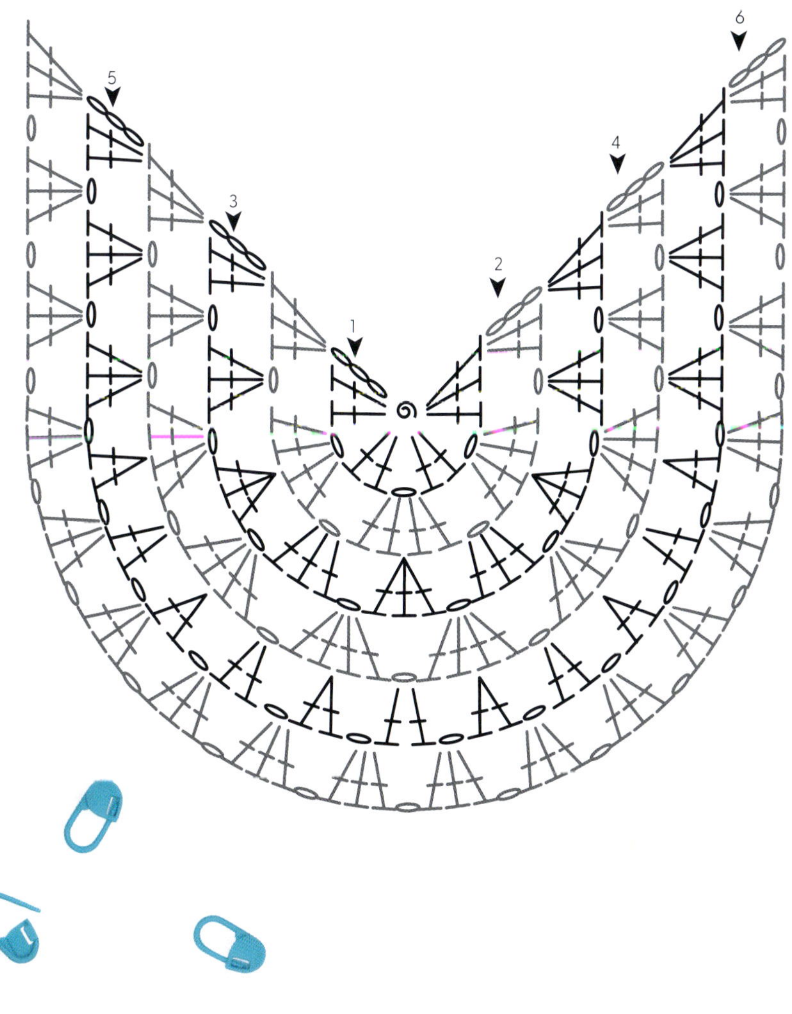

Granny #28

Teardrop

Teardrop? Flower petal? However you see this shape, it has a good point. Feeling lucky? Join four teardrops together at their points and you've got a fabulous four-leaf clover!

Instructions

Note: Work between 2nd and 3rd dc when working into 4-dc clusters.

Make magic ring.

First rnd: Ch 5 (counts 1 dc and ch-2 sp throughout), [2 dc, ch 1] 5 times in ring, 1 dc in ring; join with sl st to 3rd ch of beg ch-5.

2nd rnd: Sl st in first ch-2 sp, ch 5, 2 dc in same sp, ch 1, [4 dc, ch 1] in each ch-1 sp around, 1 dc in first ch-2 sp; join with sl st to 3rd ch of beg ch-5.

3rd rnd: Sl st in first ch-2 sp, ch 5, 2 dc in same sp, 3 dc in next ch-1 sp, ch 1, *3 dc in next 4-dcCL, ch 1, 3 dc in next ch-1 sp, ch 1, rep from * around, 1 dc in first ch-2 sp; join with sl st to 3rd ch of beg ch-5.

4th rnd: Sl st in first ch-2 sp, ch 5, 2 dc in same sp, ch 1, [4 dc, ch 1] in each ch-1 sp around, 1 dc in first ch-2 sp; join with sl st to 3rd ch of beg ch-5.

5th rnd: Sl st in first ch-2 sp, ch 5, 2 dc in same sp, ch 1, 2 dc in next ch-1 sp, ch 1, *2 dc in next 4-dcCL, ch 1, 2 dc in next ch-1 sp, ch 1, rep from * around, 1 dc in first ch-3 sp; join with sl st to 3rd ch of beg ch-5.

6th-8th rnds: Sl st in first ch-2 sp, ch 5, 2 dc in same sp, ch 1, [3 dc, ch 1] in each ch-1 sp around, 1 dc in first ch-1 sp; join with sl st to 3rd ch of beg ch-5.

To Modify

- Stop anywhere after 2nd rnd for a smaller drop (a drip?).

The Stats

- Worked in rounds
- Teardrop shape established in two rnds

Granny #29

Ornament

This one always reminds me of mid-century Christmas tree ornaments. It's an unusual shape that pieces together surprisingly well. Multiple ornaments can be seamed together easily with slip stitches (see The Finishing: All Together Now – Slip Stitch Seam).

Instructions

Make magic ring.

First rnd: Ch 4 (counts 1 dc, ch-1 sp throughout), [3 dc, ch 1] 5 times in ring, 2 dc in ring, join with sl st to 3rd ch of beg ch-4.

2nd rnd: Sl st in first ch-1 sp, ch 4, 2 dc in same ch-1 sp, ch 1, [(2 dc, ch 1) twice in next ch-1 sp] 5 times, 1 dc in first ch-1 sp, join with sl st to 3rd ch of beg ch-4.

3rd rnd: Sl st in first ch-1 sp, ch 3, 2 dc in same ch-1 sp, *3 dc in next ch-1 sp, [3 dc, 3 tr] in next ch-1 sp, sk next ch-1 sp, [3 tr, 3 dc] in next ch-1 sp, 3 dc in next ch-1 sp **, [3 dc, ch 5, 1 dc in 4th ch from hook, 1 dc in next ch, 3 dc] in next ch-1 sp; rep from * to ** once more, 3 dc in first ch-1 sp, ch 5, 1 dc in 4th ch from hook, 1 dc in next ch, join with sl st in top of beg ch-3.

Fasten off.

To Modify

- To make centre circle pop, try working stitches of 3rd rnd into back loop only of ch-1 sps, rather than into ch-1 sps.
- Glitz it up! Try holding a strand of metallic thread together with working yarn to instantly transform Ornament from basic to brilliant.

The Stats

- Worked in rnds
- Pairs well with itself and the Half Ornament

Granny #30

Half Ornament

If you're patching together a bunch of groovy Ornament shapes but don't want wavy-gravy edges, you'll find this little shape is just what you need for more straight-laced sides.

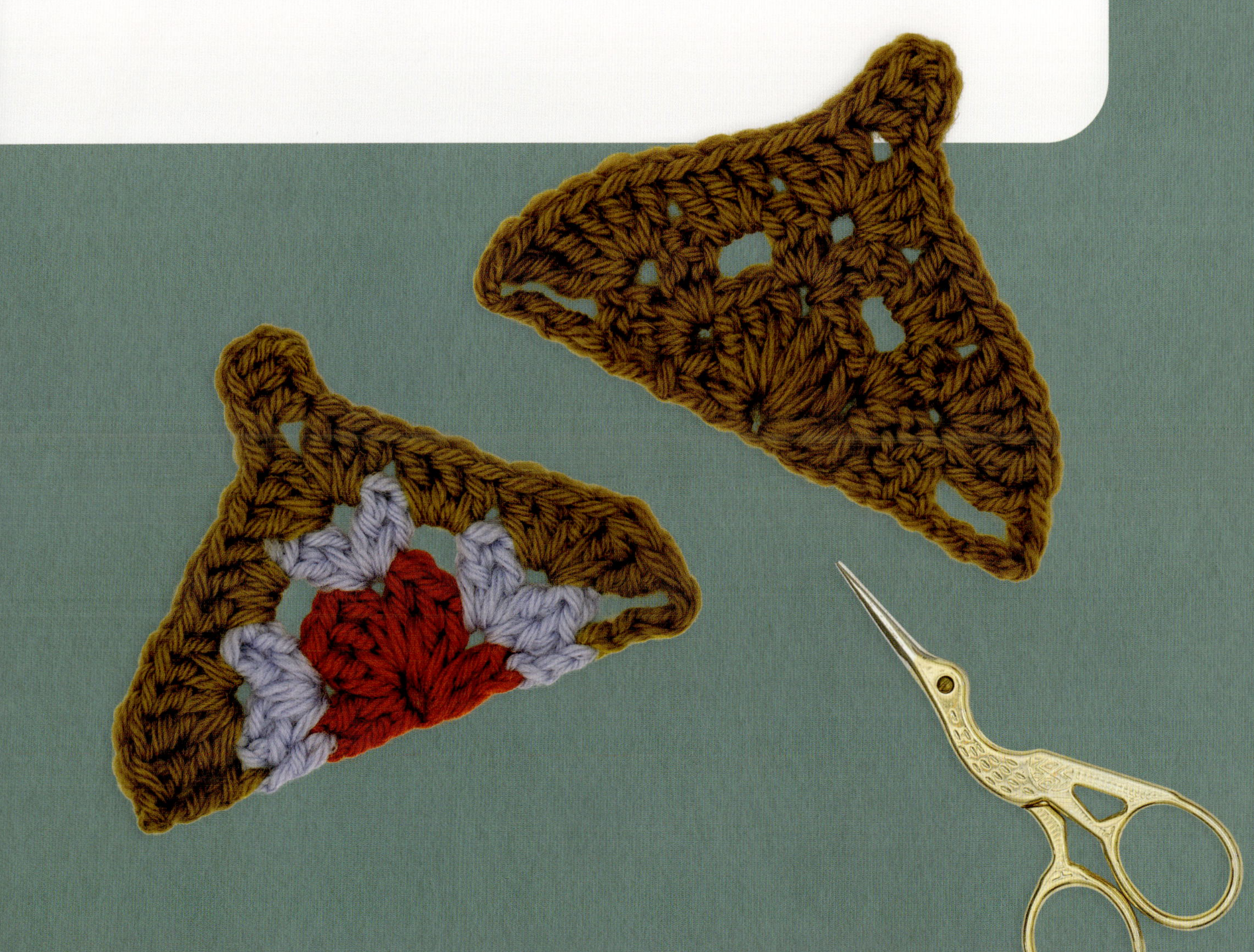

Instructions

Make magic ring.

First row: Ch 3 (counts 1 dc throughout), [1 dc, ch 1, (3 dc, ch 1) twice, 2 dc] in ring. Turn.

2nd row: Ch 3, [(2 dc, ch1) twice] in each of next 2 ch-1 sps, [2 dc, ch 1, 2 dc] in next ch-1 sp, 1 dc in top of ch-3. Turn.

3rd row: Ch 4 (counts as 1 tr), [2 tr, 3 dc] in next ch-1 sp, 3 dc in next ch-1 sp, [3 dc, ch 5, 1 dc in 4th ch from hook, 1 dc in next ch, 3 dc] in next ch-1 sp, 3 dc in next ch-1 sp, [3 dc, 2 tr] in next ch-1 sp, 1 tr in top of ch-3.

Fasten off.

To Modify

- If combining this shape with Ornament, you may want to work all rows with same side facing to match look of stitches worked in round. In this case, fasten off at end of each row, then join yarn with sl st to first stitch of prev row. All other instructions can be followed as written.

The Stats

- Worked in rows
- Pairs well with Ornament

Avoid closing the magic circle too tightly to prevent distorting the straight edge.

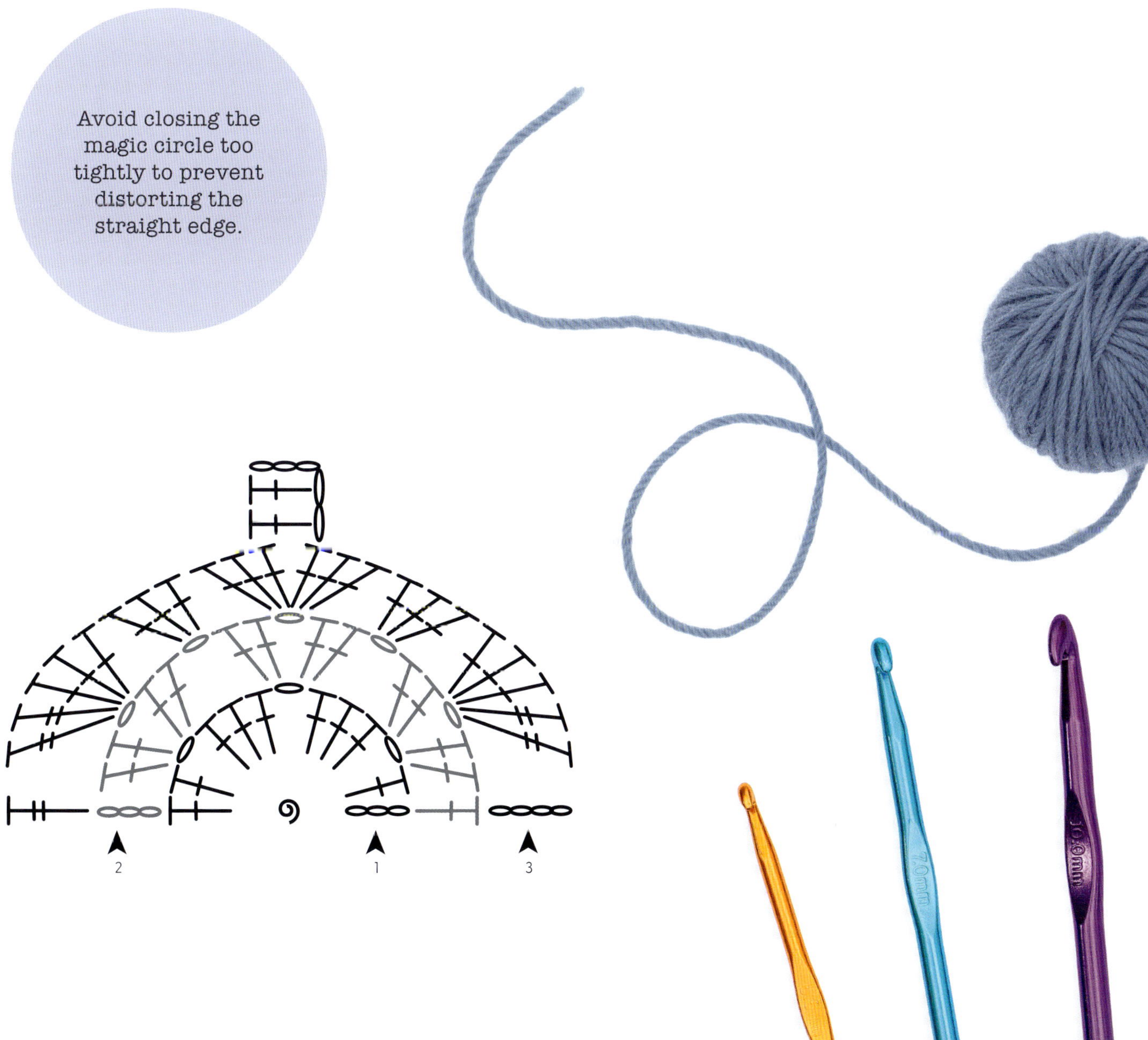

Granny #31

Leaf

You better be-leaf me when I say this quick and easy shape will help your granny garden grow! This is great add-on to the Flower and Tulip shapes - don't leaf this one behind!

Instructions

Note: Work between 2nd and 3rd dc when working into cluster.

Make magic ring

First rnd: Ch 5 (counts as 1 dc, ch-2 sp throughout), [(2 dc, ch 1) twice, 2 dc, ch 2, (2 dc, ch 1) twice,1 dc] in ring, join with sl st to 3rd ch of beg ch-5.

2nd rnd: Sl st in first ch-2 sp, ch 5, 3 dc in same ch-2 sp, ch 1, [3 dc, ch 1] in each of next 2 ch-1 sps, [3 dc, ch 2, 3 dc] in next ch-2 sp, ch 1, [3 dc, ch 1] in each of next 2 ch-1 sps, 2 dc in first ch-2 sp, join with sl st to 3rd ch of beg ch-5.

3rd rnd: Sl st in first ch-2 sp, ch 5, 4 dc in same ch-2 sp, ch 1, [4 dc, ch 1] in each of next 3 ch-1 sps, [4 dc, ch 2, 4 dc] in next ch-2 sp, ch 1, [4 dc, ch 1] in each of next 3 ch-1 sps, 3 dc in first ch-2 sp, join with sl st to 3rd ch of beg ch-5.

4th rnd: Sl st in first ch-2 sp, ch 5, 2 dc in same ch-2 sp, ch 1, [2 dc in next 4-dcCL, ch 1, 2 dc in next ch-1 sp, ch 1] 4 times, 2 dc in next 4-dcCL, ch 1, [2 dc, ch 2, 2 dc] in next ch-2 sp, ch 1, [2 dc in next 4-dcCL, ch 1, 2 dc in next ch-1 sp, ch 1] 4 times, 2 dc in next 4-dcCL, ch 1, 1 dc in first ch-2 sp, join with sl st to 3rd ch of beg ch-5.

5th rnd: Sl st in first ch-2 sp, ch 5, 3 dc in same ch-2 sp, ch 1, [3 dc, ch 1] in each ch-1 sp to next ch-2 sp, [3 dc, ch 2, 3 dc] in next ch-2 sp, ch 1, [3 dc, ch 1] in each ch-1 sp to end of rnd, 2 dc in first ch-2 sp, join with sl st to 3rd ch of beg ch-5.

To Modify

- As shape is established by end of 2nd rnd, you can stop at 2nd, 3rd or 4th rnd for smaller leaf.

The Stats

- Worked in rnds
- Re-sizeable
- Pairs well with Flower, Tulip

Granny #32

Triad

One of my favourite shirts has a print featuring this shape and I've struggled to find a name for it. Whatever you want to call it, it creates a great graphic, interlocking pattern when worked in three colours. Crocheted in three V-shaped sections, each one built on the previous, the construction is unusual but quick to memorize.

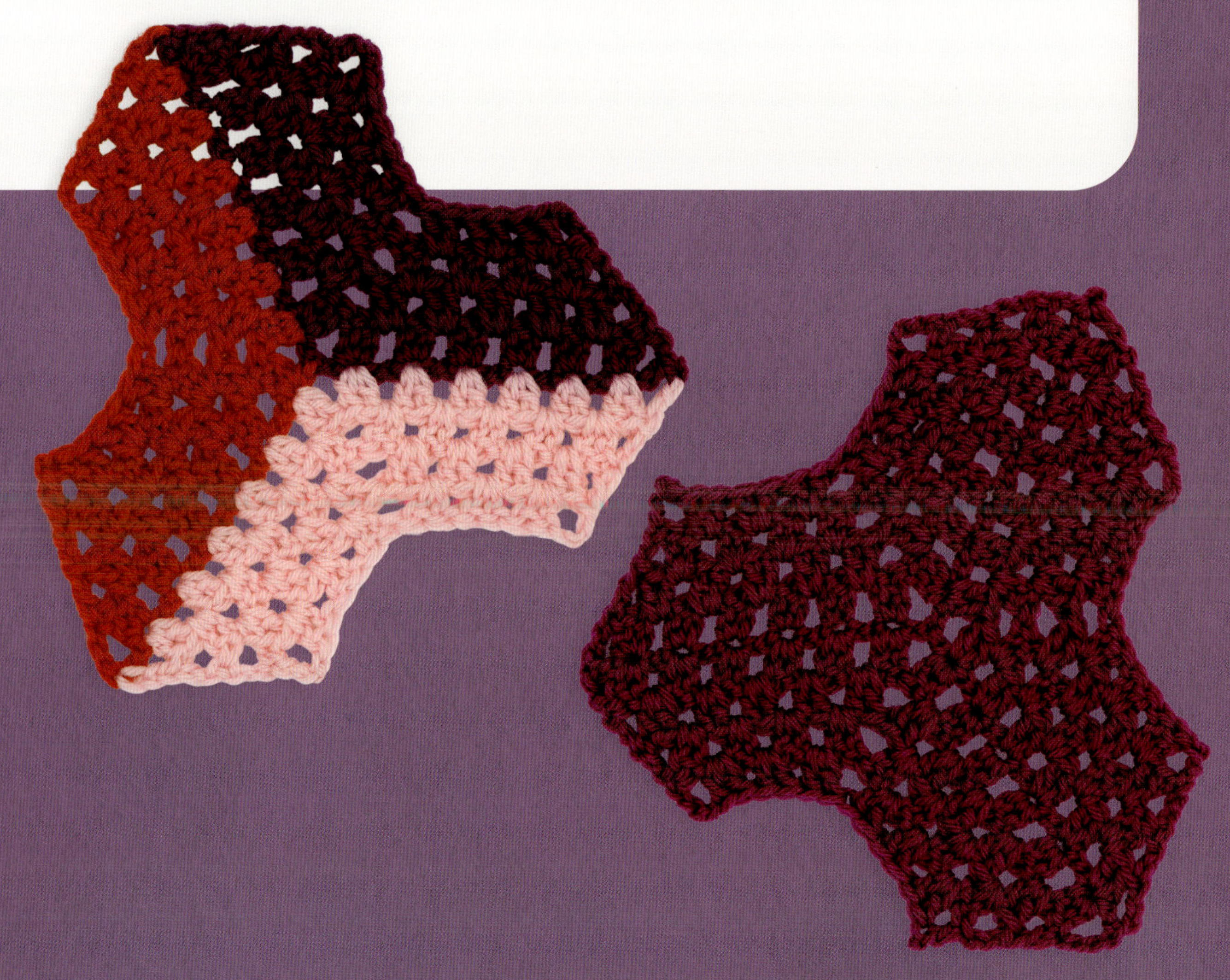

Instructions

FIRST "V"

Using A, ch 44.

First row: 2 dc in 7th ch from hook (skipped ch-6 counts as 1 dc, ch-3), [sk next 2 ch, 2 dc in next ch] 5 times, sk next 3 ch (pm on centre of these three ch), 2 dc in next ch, [sk next 2 ch, 1 dc in next ch] 5 times, sk next 2 ch, 1 dc in last ch. Turn.

From this point on, 2-dc groups will be referred to as "CL".

2nd row: Ch 3 (counts as 1 dc throughout), [2 dc between next two CLs] 5 times, sk sp between next two CLs, [2 dc between next two CLs] 5 times, 1 dc in top of ch-3. Turn.

3rd row: Ch 3, [2 dc between next two CLs] 4 times, sk sp between next two CLs, [2 dc between next two CLs] 4 times, 1 dc in top of ch-3. Turn.

4th row: Ch 3, [2 dc between next two CLs] 3 times, sk sp between next two CLs, [2 dc between next two CLs] 3 times, 1 dc in top of ch-3. Turn.

Fasten off.

SECOND "V"

Rotate First "V" 180 degrees. Join B with sl st in centre (marked) ch, ch 23.

First row: 2 dc in 7th ch from hook (skipped ch-6 counts as 1 dc, ch-3), [sk next 2 ch, 2 dc in next ch] 5 times, sk next ch, working across opposite side of foundation ch from First "V", sk next ch, 2 dc in next ch, [sk next 2 ch, 2 dc in next ch] 5 times, sk next 2 ch, 1 dc in 4th ch of skipped 6-ch. Turn.

2nd–4th rows: Using B, work 2nd–4th rows as given for First "V".

THIRD "V"

Rotate work so that rem unworked sides of First and Second "V"s foundation chains are facing up. Working across unworked side of foundation ch of First "V", join C with sl st to first ch.

First row: Ch 3, [sk next 2 ch, 2 dc in next ch] 6 times, sk next ch, working across opposite side of foundation ch from Second "V", sk next ch, 2 dc in next ch, [sk next 2 ch, 1 dc in next ch] 5 times, sk next 2 ch, 1 dc in 4th ch of skipped 6-ch. Turn.

2nd–4th rows: Using C, work 2nd–4th rows as given for First "V".

The Stats

- Worked in rows of different directions
- Best worked in three colours
- Pairs well with itself, Hexagon, Equilateral Triangle

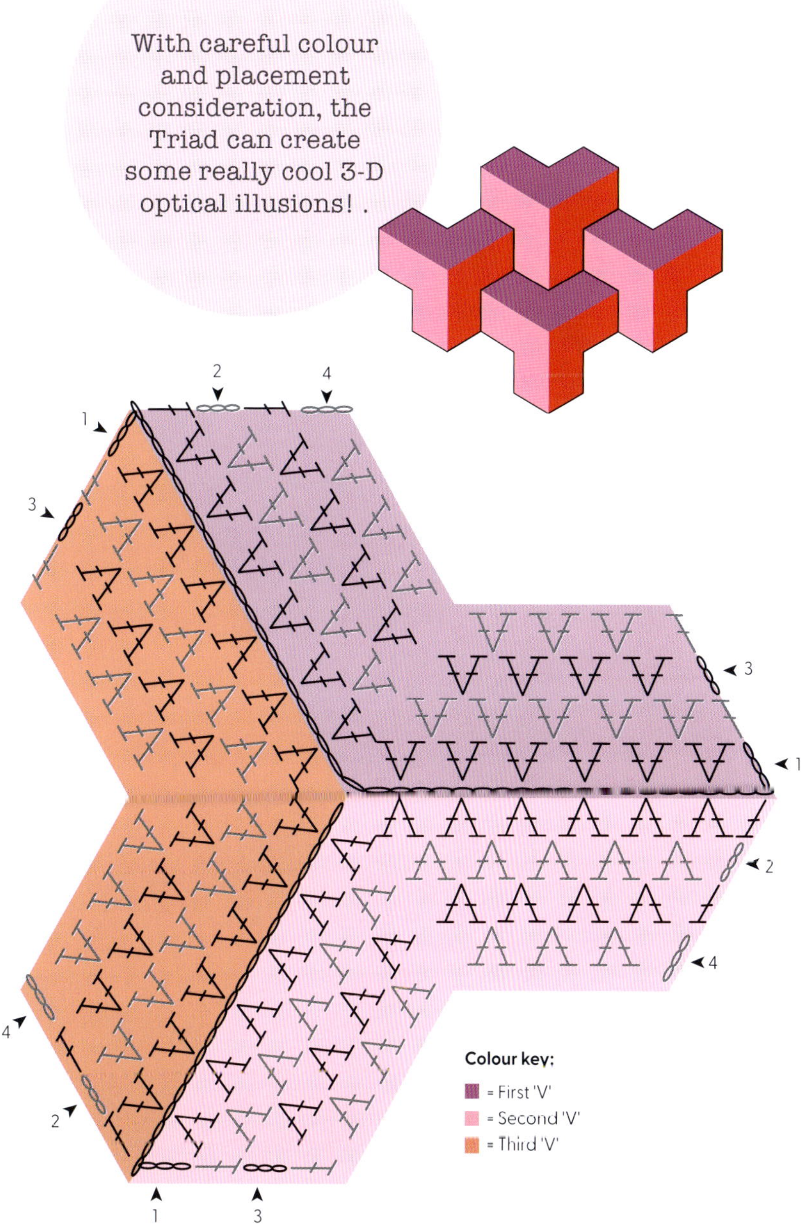

Granny #33

D*iamond

This may be the only place you will find instructions on how to grow a diamond to any size you want! If you're lookin' to piece a bunch of Diamonds together for a blanket, make sure to check out the Half Diamond Triangles 1 and 2 to fill in the sides for straight edges. Now crochet-on you crazy diamond!

Instructions

Make magic ring.

First rnd: Ch 7 (counts as 1 dc, ch-4 sp throughout), [4 dc, ch 2, 4 dc, ch 4, 4 dc, ch 2, 3 dc] in ring, join with sl st to 3rd ch of beg ch-7.

2nd rnd: Sl st in first 2 ch, ch 7, 4 dc in same ch-4 sp, ch 2, [3 dc, ch 2, 3 dc] in next ch-2 sp, ch 2, [4 dc, ch 4, 4 dc] in next ch-4 sp, ch 2, [3 dc, ch 2, 3 dc] in next ch-2 sp, ch 2, 3 dc in first ch-4 sp, join with sl st to 3rd ch of beg ch-7.

3rd rnd: Sl st in first 2 ch, ch 7, 4 dc in same ch-4 sp, *ch 2, 4 dc in next ch-2 sp, ch 2, [1 dc, ch 2, 1 dc] in next corner ch-2 sp, ch 2, 4 dc in next ch-2 sp, ch 2 **, [4 dc, ch 4, 4 dc] in next corner ch-4 sp; rep from * to **, 3 dc in first ch-4 sp, join with sl st to 3rd ch of beg ch-7.

4th rnd: Sl st in first 2 ch, ch 7, 4 dc in same ch-4 sp, *[ch 2, 4 dc] in each ch-2 sp to next corner ch-2 sp, ch 4, sk corner ch-2 sp, [4 dc, ch 2] in each ch-2 sp to next corner ch-4 sp**, [4 dc, ch 4, 4 dc] in corner ch-4 sp, rep from * to **, 3 dc in first ch-4 sp, join with sl st to 3rd ch of beg ch-7.

5th rnd: Sl st in first 2 ch, ch 7, 4 dc in same ch-4 sp, *ch 2, [4 dc, ch 2] in each ch-2 sp to next corner ch-4 sp, [3 dc, ch 2, 3 dc] in corner ch-4 sp, ch 2, [4 dc, ch 2] in each ch-2 sp to next ch-4 sp **, [4 dc, ch 4, 4 dc] in next ch-4 sp; rep from * to **, 3 dc in first ch-4 sp, join with sl st to 3rd ch of beg ch-7.

6th rnd: Sl st in first 2 ch, ch 7, 4 dc in same ch-4 sp, *ch 2, [4 dc, ch 2] in each ch-2 sp to next corner ch-2 sp, [1 dc, ch 2, 1 dc] in next ch-2 sp, ch 2, [4 dc, ch 2] in each ch-2 sp to next corner ch-4 sp **, [4 dc, ch 4, 4 dc] in next corner ch-4 sp; rep from * to **, 3 dc in first ch-4 sp, join with sl st to 3rd ch of beg ch-7.

To Modify

- Rep 4th–6th rnds to desired dimensions.
- Bring points of six diamonds together and you've got yourself a star!

The Stats

- Worked in rnds
- Infinite growth potential
- Pairs well with Half Diamond Triangles 1 or 2

Granny #34

Pentagon

It's no surprise that the building housing the U.S. Department of Defense is "the Pentagon": this five-sided shape is somewhat defensive. It's easy enough to crochet a granny pentagon, but unlike the pedestrian square or the sexy hex-y, this pent-up polygon isn't easy to match up with other shapes. Regardless, it's perfectly nice on its own so why not try a five-sided blanket for a change?

Instructions

Make magic ring.

First rnd: Ch 5 (counts as 1 dc, ch-2 sp throughout), [3 dc, ch 2] 4 times in ring, 2 dc in ring, join with sl st to 3rd ch of beg ch-5.

2nd rnd: Sl st in first ch-2 sp, ch 5, 3 dc, in same ch-2 sp, [3 dc, ch 2, 3 dc] in each ch-2 around, 2 dc in first ch-2 sp, join with sl st to 3rd ch of beg ch-5.

3rd rnd: Sl st in first ch-2 sp, ch 5, 3 dc in same ch-2 sp, [3 dc between next two 3-dcCLs, (3 dc, ch 2, 3 dc) in next ch-2 sp] 4 times, 3 dc between next two 3-dcCLs, 2 dc in first ch-2 sp, join with sl st to 3rd ch of beg ch-5.

4th rnd: Sl st in first ch-2 sp, ch 5, 3 dc in same ch-2 sp, [3 dc between next two 3-dcCLs to next corner ch-2 sp, (3 dc, ch 2, 3 dc) in corner ch-2 sp] 4 times, 3 dc between next two 3-dcCLs to first corner ch-2 sp, 2 dc in first corner ch-2 sp, join with sl st to 3rd ch of beg ch-5.

To Modify

- Rep 4th rnd to desired size. If your Pentagon starts getting a little ripple-y and doesn't want to lie flat, try working [2 dc, ch 2, 2 dc] corners every second round or so.

The Stats

- Worked in rnds
- Infinite growth potential
- Pairs well with itself

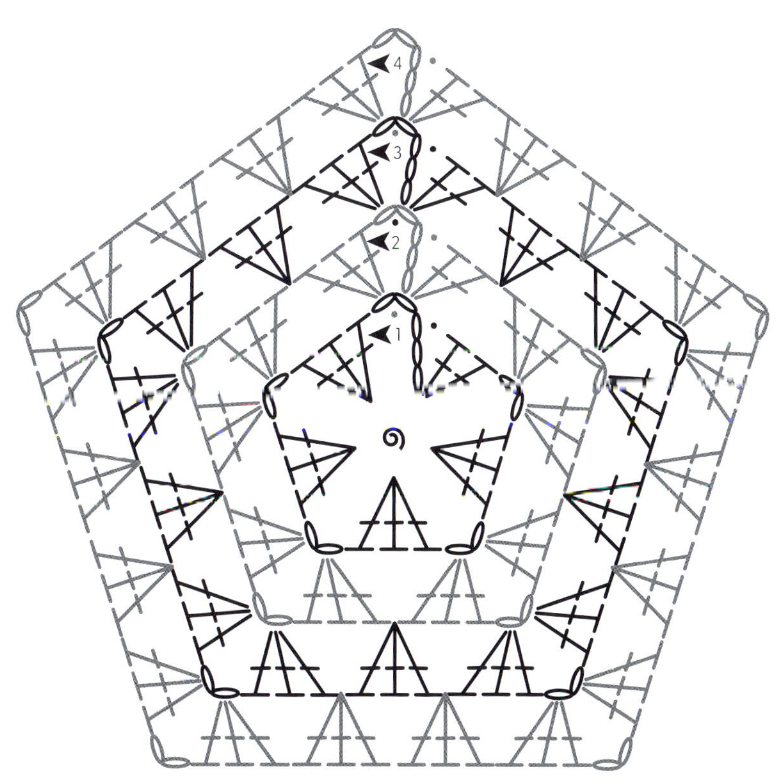

Granny #35

Hexagon

This popular variation of the Classic Granny square is the bee's knees! Hexagon motifs make beautiful patchwork pieces and combined with half hexagons, you can easily straighten out the exterior edges. It's worth noting that this version of a granny hexagon strays from the typical 3-dc-ch-1 pattern but the result is a hexagon that will lie flat at any size.

Instructions

Make magic ring.

First rnd: Ch 5 (counts as 1 dc, ch-2 sp throughout), [2 dc, ch 2] 5 times in ring, 1 dc in ring, join with sl st to 3rd ch of beg ch-5.

2nd rnd: Sl st in first ch-2 sp, ch 5, 2 dc in same ch-2 sp, [2 dc, ch 2, 2 dc] in each ch-1 sp around, 1 dc in first ch-2 sp, join with sl st to 3rd ch of beg ch-5.

From this point on, 2-dc groups will be referred to as "CLs".

3rd rnd: Sl st in first ch-2 sp, ch 5, 2 dc in same ch-2 sp, 2 dc between next two CLs, *[2 dc, ch 2, 2 dc] in next ch-2 sp, 2 dc between next two CLs; rep from * around, 1 dc in first ch-2 sp, join with sl st to 3rd ch of beg ch-5.

4th rnd: Sl st in first ch-2 sp, ch 5, 2 dc in same ch-2 sp, [2 dc between next two CLs] to next ch-2 sp, *[2 dc, ch 2, 2 dc] in next ch-2 sp, [2 dc between next two CLs] to next ch-2 sp; rep from * around, 1 dc in first ch-2 sp, join with sl st to 3rd ch of beg ch-5.

To Modify

- Rep 4th rnd to desired size.
- Corners too pointy or work starting to ripple? Try working [hdc, ch 2, hdc] in each ch-2 corner space on every second round or so for fine-tuning. Remember to make the same adjustments to any Half Hexagons if working the shapes together.

The Stats

- Worked in rnds
- Infinite growth potential
- Pairs well with Half Hexagon 1 or 2

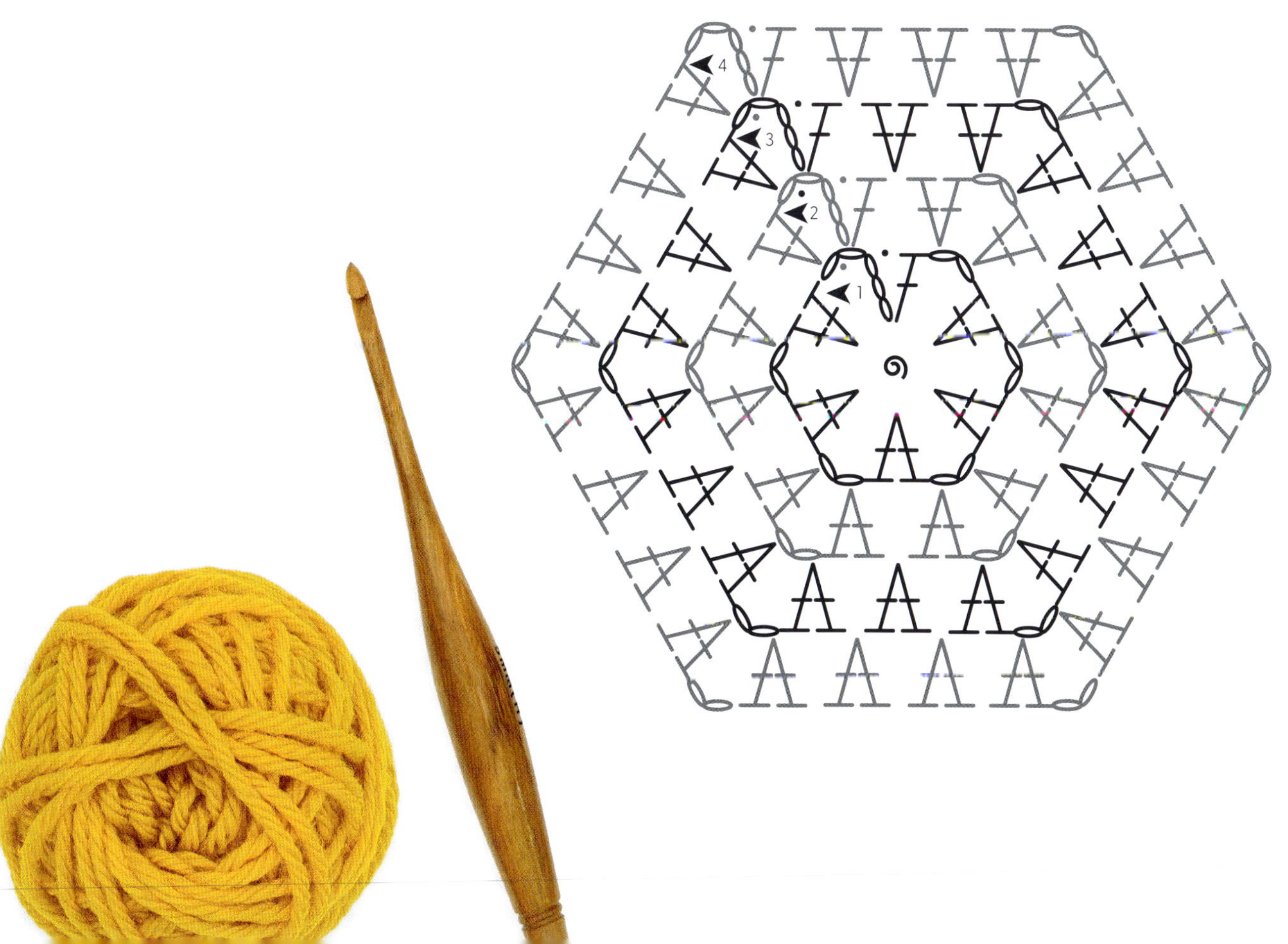

Granny #36

Half Hexagon 1

Let's go halfsies! When piecing a series of hexagons together, you can find yourself with some wonky edges. Maybe that's the look you're going for, but if you prefer to go straight-edge, the Half Hexagon is your new best friend: great for filling in gaps, and not half-bad on its own! There's more than one way to half a hexie, so check out the Half Hexagon 2 too!

Instructions

Make magic ring.

First row: Ch 3 (counts as 1 dc throughout), [1 dc, ch 2, 2 dc, ch 2, 2 dc] in ring. Turn.

2nd row: Ch 3, 1 dc in first dc, [2 dc, ch 2, 2 dc] in each of next two ch-2 sps, 2 dc in top of ch-3. Turn.

From this point on, 2-dc groups will be referred to as "CLs".

3rd row: Ch 3, 1 dc in first dc, [2 dc between next two CLs, (2 dc, ch 2, 2 dc) in next ch-2 sp] twice, 2 dc between next two CLs, 2 dc in top of ch-3. Turn.

4th row: Ch 3, 1 dc in first dc, [(2 dc between next two CLs) to next ch-2 sp, (2 dc, ch 2, 2 dc) in next ch-2 sp] twice, [2 dc between next two CLs] to last CL, 2 dc in top of ch-3. Turn.

To Modify

* Rep 4th row to desired size.

The Stats

* Worked in rows
* Infinite growth potential
* Pairs well with Hexagon, Half Hexagon 2

Granny #37

Half Hexagon 2

You know how you can cut a sandwich side-to-side or corner to corner? You've got the same options with the Half Hexagon. Wanna make a hexagon-patched blanket with straight edges? You'll find you need both The Half Hexagon 1 and 2 no matter how you slice it.

Instructions

Make magic ring.

First row: Ch 5 (counts as 1 dc, ch-2 sp throughout), [(2 dc, ch 2) twice, 1 dc] in ring. Turn.

2nd row: Ch 3 (counts as 1 dc throughout), [1 dc, ch 2, 2 dc] in first ch-2 sp, [2 dc, ch 2, 2 dc] in next ch-2 sp, [2 dc, ch 2, 1 dc] in next ch-2 sp, 1 dc in 3rd ch of ch-5. Turn.

From this point on, 2-dc groups will be referred to as "CLs".

3rd row: Ch 3, [(2 dc, ch 2, 2 dc) in next ch-2 sp, 2 dc between next two CLs] twice, [2 dc, ch 2, 2 dc] in next ch-2 sp, 1 dc in top of ch-3. Turn.

4th row: Ch 3, 1 dc between first dc and first CL, [2 dc, ch 2, 2 dc] in next ch-2 sp, [(2 dc between next two CLs) twice, (2 dc, ch 2, 2 dc) in next ch-2 sp] twice, 1 dc between last CL and ch-3, 1 dc in top of ch-3. Turn.

5th row: Ch 3, [2 dc between next two CLs] to next ch-2 sp, (2 dc, ch 2, 2 dc) in next ch-2 sp] 3 times, 2 dc between next two CLs to end of row, 1 dc in top of ch-3. Turn.

6th row: Ch 3, 1 dc between first dc and first CL, [(2 dc between next two CLs) to next ch-2 sp, (2 dc, ch 2, 2 dc) in next ch-2 sp] 3 times, [2 dc between next two CLs] to end of row, 1 dc between last CL and ch-3, 1 dc in top of ch-3. Turn.

The Stats

- Worked in rows
- Infinite growth potential
- Pairs well with Hexagon, Half Hexagon 1

To Modify

- Rep 5th and 6th rows to desired size.

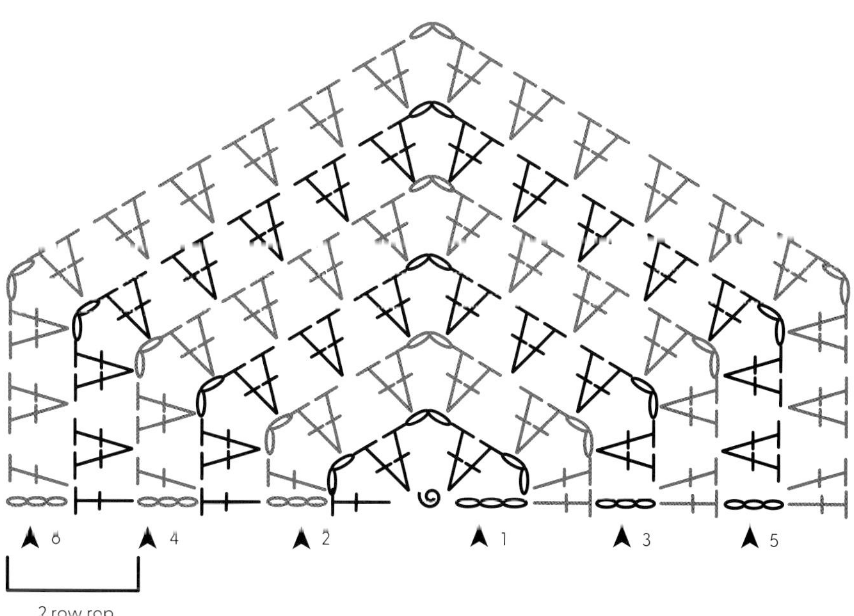

Granny #38

Octagon

The Octagon takes the award for “most sides on a granny” (at least in this book: anything more than eight sides and you’re basically making a circle as far as I’m concerned).

Instructions

Make magic ring.

First rnd: Ch 4 (counts as 1 dc, ch-1 sp throughout), [2 dc, ch 1] 7 times in ring, 1 dc in ring, join with sl st to 3rd ch of beg ch-4.

2nd rnd: Sl st in first ch-1 sp, ch 3 (counts as 1 dc throughout), 2 dc in same ch-1 sp, ch 1, [3 dc, ch 1] in each ch-1 sp around, join with sl st in top of beg ch-3.

3rd rnd: Ch 3, 1 dc in first dc, ch 1, sk next dc, 2 dc in next dc, ch 1, *2 dc in next dc, ch 1, sk next dc, 2 dc in next dc, ch 1; rep from * around, join with sl st in top of beg ch-3.

4th rnd: Ch 4, sk next dc, 3 dc in next ch-1 sp, ch 1, sk next dc, 1 dc in next dc, ch 1, *1 dc in next dc, ch 1, 3 dc in next ch-1 sp, ch 1, sk next dc, 1 dc in next dc, ch 1; rep from * around, join with sl st to 3rd ch of beg ch-4.

5th rnd: Ch 3, 3 dc in first ch-1 sp, ch 1, 3 dc in next ch-1 sp, 1 dc in next dc, ch 1, *1 dc in next dc, 3 dc in next ch-1 sp, ch 1, 3 dc in next ch-1 sp, 1 dc in next dc, ch 1; rep from * around, join with sl st in top of beg ch-3.

6th rnd: Ch 3, 2 dc in first dc, ch 1, 3 dc in next ch-1 sp, ch 1, sk next 3 dc, 3 dc in next dc, ch 1 (PM on ch for corner), *3 dc in next dc, ch 1, 3 dc in next ch-1 sp, ch 1, sk next 3 dc, 3 dc in next dc, ch 1 (PM on ch for corner); rep from * around, join with sl st in top of beg ch-3.

Move marker each rnd to new corner sp.

7th rnd: Ch 3, 1 dc in first dc, ch 1 [3 dc, ch 1] in each ch-1 sp to next corner, 2 dc in last dc before corner, ch 1 (corner), *2 dc in next dc, ch 1, [3 dc, ch 1] in each ch-1 sp to next corner, 2 dc in last dc before corner, ch-1 (corner); rep from * around, join with sl st in top of ch-3.

8th rnd: Ch 4, sk next dc, [3 dc, ch 1] in each ch-1 sp to next corner, 1 dc in last dc before corner, ch 1 (corner), *1 dc in next dc, ch 1, [3 dc, ch 1] in each ch-1 sp to next corner, 1 dc in last dc before corner, ch 1 (corner); rep from * around, join with sl st to 3rd ch of beg ch-4.

9th rnd: Ch 3, 3 dc in first ch-1 sp, [ch 1, 3 dc] in each ch-1 sp to next corner, 1 dc in last dc before corner, ch 1 (corner), *1 dc in next dc, 3 dc in next ch-1 sp, [ch 1, 3 dc] in each ch-1 sp to next corner, 1 dc in last dc before corner, ch 1 (corner); rep from * around, join with sl st in top of beg ch-3.

10th rnd: Ch 3, 2 dc in first dc, ch 1, [3 dc, ch 1] in each ch-1 sp to next corner, 3 dc in last dc before corner, ch 1 (corner), *3 dc in next dc, ch I, [3 dc, ch 1] in each ch-1 sp to next corner, 3 dc in last dc before corner, ch 1 (corner); rep from * around, join with sl st in top of beg ch-3.

To Modify

- Rep 7th–10th rnds to desired size.
- While sharp octagon shape isn't clear until 5th or 6th rnd, you can block to an octagon after any rnd.
- Use of markers is optional as you may find it easy enough to distinguish corners without them.
- For more defined corners, work ch-2 instead of ch-1 on last rnd.

The Stats

- Worked in rnds
- Infinite growth potential
- Shape established after 5th rnd
- Pairs well with any square, Half Square Triangle 1 or 2

The octagon combines nicely with squares

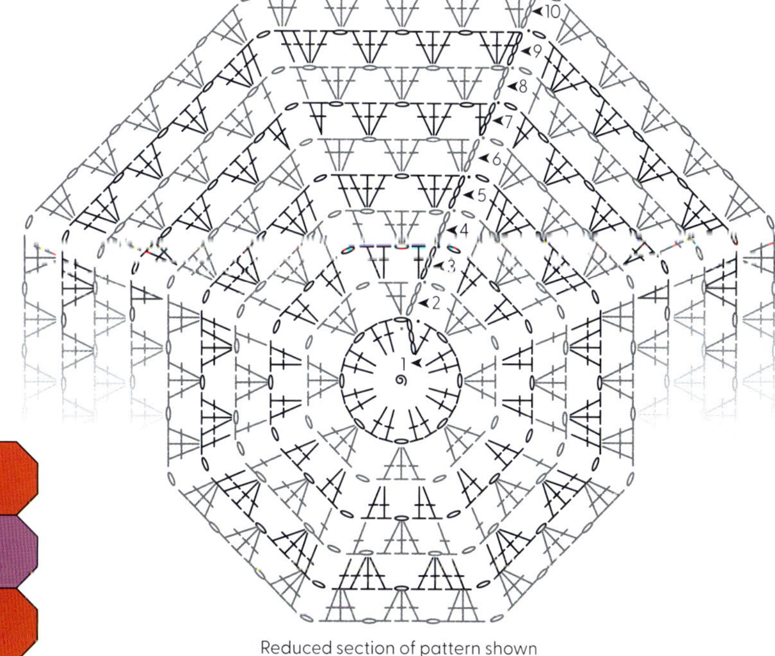

Reduced section of pattern shown

Granny #39

Zig-Zag

Zig-zag, chevron, peaks and valleys, whatever you choose to call it, this one is a classic. This pattern makes a top-notch blanket, but can also be used in combination with squares and triangles to great effect.

Instructions

Ch 51 (multiple of 24 plus 3, minimum of 51).

First row: 3 dc in 7th ch from hook (skipped ch-6 counts as 1 dc, sk ch-3), ch 1, sk next 3 ch, 3 dc in next ch, ch 1, sk next 3 ch, [3 dc, ch 2, 3 dc] in next ch (peak), ch 1, sk next 3 ch, 3 dc in next ch, ch 1, sk next 3 ch, *3 dc in next ch, sk next 7 ch (valley), 3 dc in next ch, ch 1, sk next 3 ch, 3 dc in next ch, ch 1, sk next 3 ch, [3 dc, ch 2, 3 dc] in next ch (peak), ch 1, sk next 3 ch, 3 dc in next ch, ch 1, sk next 3 ch; rep from * to last 5 ch, 3 dc in next ch, sk next 3 ch, 1 dc in last ch. Turn.

2nd row: Ch 3 (counts as 1 dc), [3 dc in next ch-1 sp, ch 1] to next ch-2 sp, [3 dc, ch 2, 3 dc] in next ch-2 sp (peak), [ch 1, 3 dc in next ch-1 sp] to next valley (where there is no ch-1 between two 3-dcCLs), *sk next two 3-dcCLs, [3 dc in next ch-1 sp, ch 1] to next ch-2 sp, [3 dc, ch 2, 3 dc in next ch-2 sp] (peak), [ch 1, 3 dc in next ch-1 sp] to next valley; rep from * to last st, 1 dc in top of ch-3. Turn.

To Modify

- Rep 2nd row to desired length.
- Two methods to add width:

  1. To create additional peaks and valleys, add 24 ch to foundation chain for each additional peak and valley. Will add width without adding height to each chevron.

  2. For more length between each peak and valley, add multiples of 8 to foundation chain: 8 ch for each "peak" in row. For example, pattern as written with foundation chain of 51 has total of 2 peaks. To add one more CL between each peak and valley, add 16 to foundation chain, making it 67. This creates a taller chevron and adds both width and height.

The Stats

- Worked in rows
- Infinite growth potential
- Adjustable chevron width
- Pairs well with any square, Half Square Triangle 1 or 2

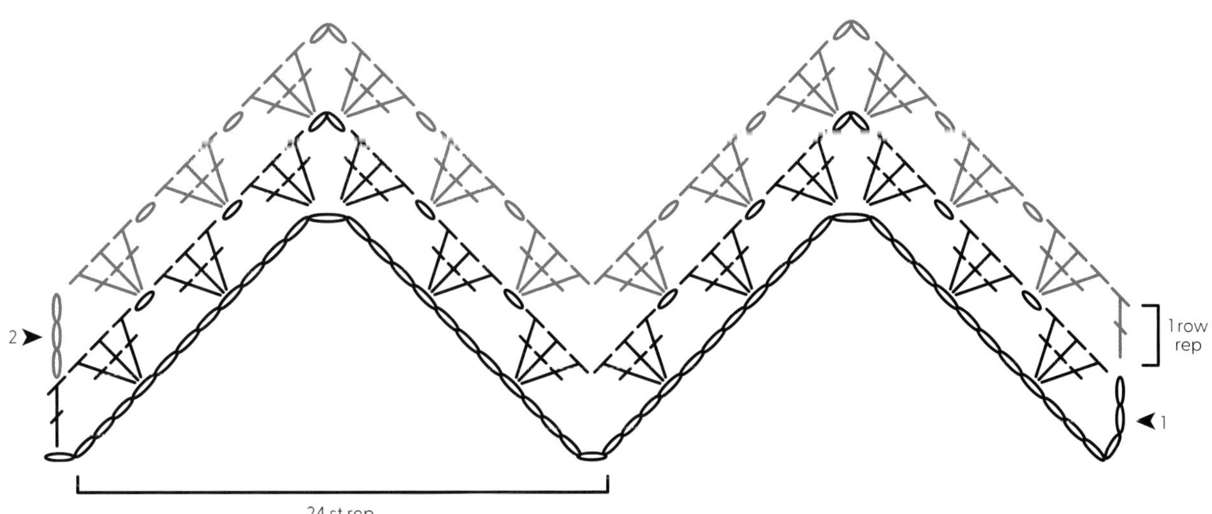

Granny #40

Trapezoid*

I like to think of the trapezoid as a "flare square". Trapezoids fit together in rows nicely for extra flair (see what I did there?) in a blanket, or a dozen would work together to form a ring. Play around and see what designs you can come up with!

Instructions

Make magic ring.

First rnd: Ch 5 (counts as 1 dc, ch-2 sp throughout), [3 dc, ch 2, 4 dc, ch 2, 3 dc, ch 2, 1 dc] in ring, join with sl st to 3rd ch of beg ch-5.

2nd rnd: Sl st in first ch-2 sp, ch 5, 3 dc in same ch-2 sp, ch 1, [3 dc, ch 2, 4 dc] in next ch-2 sp, ch 1, [4 dc, ch 2, 3 dc] in next ch-2 sp, ch 1, [3 dc, ch 2, 2 dc] in next ch-2 sp, ch 1, 1 dc in first ch-2 sp, join with sl st to 3rd ch of beg ch-5.

3rd rnd: Sl st in first ch-2 sp, ch 5, 3 dc in same ch-2 sp, ch 1, 3 dc in next ch-1 sp, ch 1, [3 dc, ch 2, 4 dc] in next ch-2 sp, ch 1, 4 dc in next ch-1 sp, ch 1, [4 dc, ch 2, 3 dc] in next ch-2 sp, ch 1, 3 dc in next ch-1 sp, ch 1, [3 dc, ch 2, 2 dc] in next ch-2 sp, ch 1, 2 dc in next ch-1 sp, ch 1, 1 dc in first ch-2 sp, join with sl st to 3rd ch of beg ch-5.

4th rnd: Sl st in first ch-2 sp, ch 5, 3 dc in same ch-2 sp, [ch 1, 3 dc] in each ch-1 sp to next corner ch-2 sp, ch 1, [3 dc, ch 2, 4 dc] in next ch-2 sp, [ch 1, 4 dc] in each ch-1 sp to next corner ch-2 sp, ch 1, [4 dc, ch 2, 3 dc] in next ch-2 sp, [ch 1, 3 dc] in each ch-1 sp to next corner ch-2 sp, ch 1, [3 dc, ch 2, 2 dc] in next ch-2 sp, [ch 1, 2 dc] in each ch-1 sp to first corner ch-2 sp, ch 1, 1 dc in first ch-2 sp, join with sl st to 3rd ch of beg ch-5.

To Modify

* Rep 4th rnd to desired size.
* If 12 Trapezoids are joined together side-to-side to form a ring, the centre space will be near-enough to a smooth circle to be filled in with the Simple Circle.

The Stats

* Worked in rnds
* Infinite growth potential
* Pairs well with itself, any square, Simple Circle

Granny #41

Boot

If a granny triangle and granny rectangle had a baby, it would be what I call the granny "Boot". This handy little shape can be used for necklines or armhole shaping in a garment, or works as an unusual shape to spice up a patchwork project. The length of the "leg" of the boot can be adjusted to almost any size, making it easy to use in combination with other straight-sided shapes.

Instructions

Ch 13 (multiple of 4 plus 1).

1st row: [3 dc, ch 2, 3 dc] in 5th ch from hook (skipped ch-4 counts as 1 dc, ch-1 sp) ch 1, sk next 3 ch, *3 dc in next ch, ch 1, sk next 3 ch; rep from * to last ch, 2 dc in last ch. Turn.

2nd row: Ch 3 (counts as 1 dc throughout), [3 dc in next ch-1 sp, ch 1] to next corner ch-2 sp, [3 dc, ch 2, 3 dc] in corner ch-2 sp, ch 1, 3 dc in last ch-4 sp, ch 1, 1 dc in 3rd ch of ch-4. Turn.

3rd row: Ch 4 (counts as 1 dc, ch-1 sp throughout), 3 dc in first ch-1 sp, ch 1, [3 dc in next ch-1 sp, ch 1] to corner ch-2 sp, [3 dc, ch 2, 3 dc] in corner ch-2 sp, ch 1, [3 dc in next ch-1 sp, ch 1] to last st, 2 dc in top of ch-3. Turn.

4th row: Ch 3, [3 dc in next ch-1 sp, ch 1] to corner ch-2 sp, [3 dc, ch 2, 3 dc] in corner ch-2 sp, ch 1, [3 dc in next ch-1 sp, ch 1] to last ch-4 sp, 3 dc in last ch-4 sp, ch 1, 1 dc in 3rd ch of ch-4. Turn.

To Modify

- Rep 3rd and 4th rows to desired size.
- To create Boot with a "sole" the same measure as Classic Granny Square, match number of "Boot" rows to number of square rnds.
- To lengthen or shorten "leg" of Boot, add or subtract multiple of 4 when making foundation chain.

The Stats

- Worked in rows
- Adjustable dimensions
- Infinite growth potential
- Reversible
- Pairs well with Classic Granny, any rectangle, Half Square Triangle 1 or 2

Working the first row of stitches into the "back bump" of the foundation chain will leave both loops of the chain free for seaming.

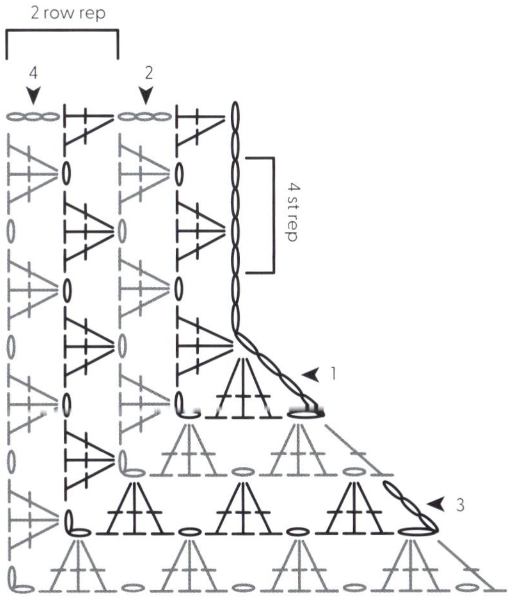

2 row rep
4
2
4 st rep
1
3

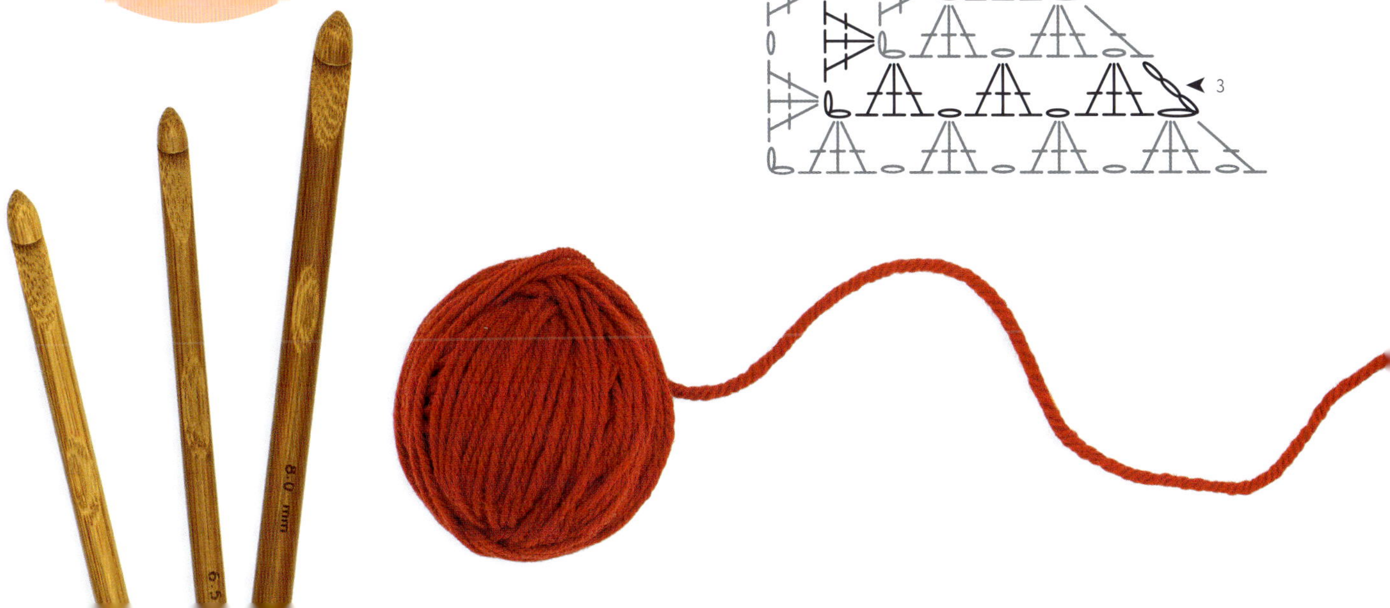

Granny #42

Small Five-Point Star

Twinkle, twinkle, five-point star, what an easy craft you are! This little guy is completed with just three rounds. Perfect for Christmas tree ornaments, or anywhere you want to add a little star power.

These little stars can be slip-stitched together at their points using the Join-As-You-Go technique.

Instructions

Make magic ring.

First rnd: Ch 5 (counts as 1 dc, ch-2 sp throughout), [3 dc, ch 2] 4 times in ring, 2 dc in ring, join with sl st to 3rd ch of beg ch-5.

2nd rnd: Sl st in first ch-2 sp, ch 5, 3 dc, in same ch-2 sp, [3 dc, ch 2, 3 dc] in each ch-2 sp around, 2 dc in first ch-2 sp, join with sl st to 3rd ch of beg ch-5.

3rd rnd: Sl st in first ch-2 sp, ch 6 (counts as 1 dc, ch-3 sp), 3 dc in same ch-2 sp, ch 2, sl st between next two 3-dcCLs, *ch 2, [3 dc, ch 3, 3 dc] in next ch-2 sp, ch 2, sl st between next two 3-dcCLs; rep from * around, ch 2, 2 dc in first ch-2 sp, join with sl st to 3rd ch of beg ch-6.

Fasten off.

To Modify

- Bigger stars in your eyes? Check out Any Size Five-Point Star.

The Stats

- Worked in rnds
- Pairs well with itself

Granny #43

Any Size Five-Point Star

Here's a formula for a classic five-point star you can reconfigure to any size you like, from dishcloth to big-'ole blanket. The secret? This star is simply a pentagon with some triangles added for flair!

Instructions

Base Pentagon: Make Base Pentagon as Pentagon, with minimum of 2 rnds (see *). Sl st in first corner ch-2 sp. Turn.

FIRST POINT

First row (WS): Ch 3 (counts as 1 dc throughout), [3 dc between next two 3-dcCLs] to next ch-2 sp, 1 dc in ch-2 sp. Turn.

2nd row (RS): Ch 3, [3 dc between next two 3-dcCL] to last st, 1 dc in top of ch-3, turn.

*__Begin here if starting with 2-rnd Pentagon__

If Base Pentagon has more than 4 rnds, rep 2nd row until 2 CLs remain.

3rd row: Ch 3, 3 dc between next two CLs, 1 dc in top of ch-3, turn.

4th row: Ch 3, dc2tog over centre dc of 3 dcCL and in top of ch-3.

Fasten off.

SECOND THROUGH FIFTH POINTS

With WS facing, join yarn with sl st to next unworked ch-2 sp of last rnd of Base Pentagon

Work all rows as given for First Point.

To Modify

- To enlarge, simply work more rnds of Base Pentagon before working points.
- For a tinier twinkle, see Small Five-Point Star.
- For perfectionists (no judgment, I count myself among you!), work join-&-turn rnds for Base Pentagon to match look of fabric when switching to rows to work points.

The Stats

- Worked in rnds and rows
- Infinite growth potential

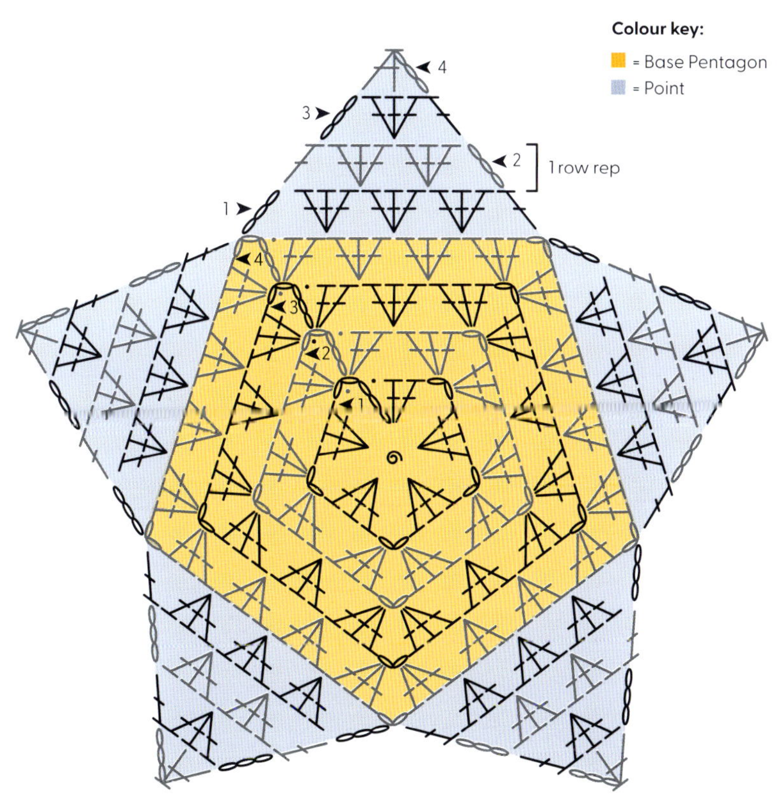

Granny #44

Six-Point Star

There are almost as many ways to crochet a star as there are points of light in the night sky. This granny star has something that most patterns don't: it can be made as large as you like. Simply add some points to a hexagon and a star is born!

Instructions

Base Hexagon: Make Base Hexagon as Hexagon, with minimum of 2 rnds (see *). Sl st in first ch-2 sp. Turn.

FIRST POINT

From this point on, 2-dc groups of Base Hexagon will be referred to as "CLs".

First row: Ch 3 (counts as 1 dc throughout), [2 dc between next two CLs] to next ch-2 sp, 1 dc in ch-2 sp. Turn.

2nd row: Ch 3, [2 dc between next two CLs] to last st, 1 dc in top of ch-3. Turn.

*__Begin here if starting with 2-rnd Hexagon__

If Base Hexagon has more than 4 rnds, rep 2nd row until two CLs remain.

3rd row: Ch 3, 2 dc between next two CLs, 1 dc in top of ch-3. Turn.

4th row: Ch 3, 1 dc in top of ch-3.

Fasten off.

SECOND THROUGH SIXTH POINTS

With WS facing, join yarn with sl st to next unworked ch-2 sp of last rnd of Base Hexagon.

Work first–4th rows as given for First Point.

To Modify

- To enlarge, simply work more rnds of Base Hexagon before working points.
- For perfectionists (no judgment, I count myself among you!), work join-&-turn rnds for Base Hexagon to match look of fabric when switching to rows to work points.

The Stats

- Worked in rnds, then rows
- Infinite growth potential
- Pairs well with the Parallelogram and Equilateral Triangle

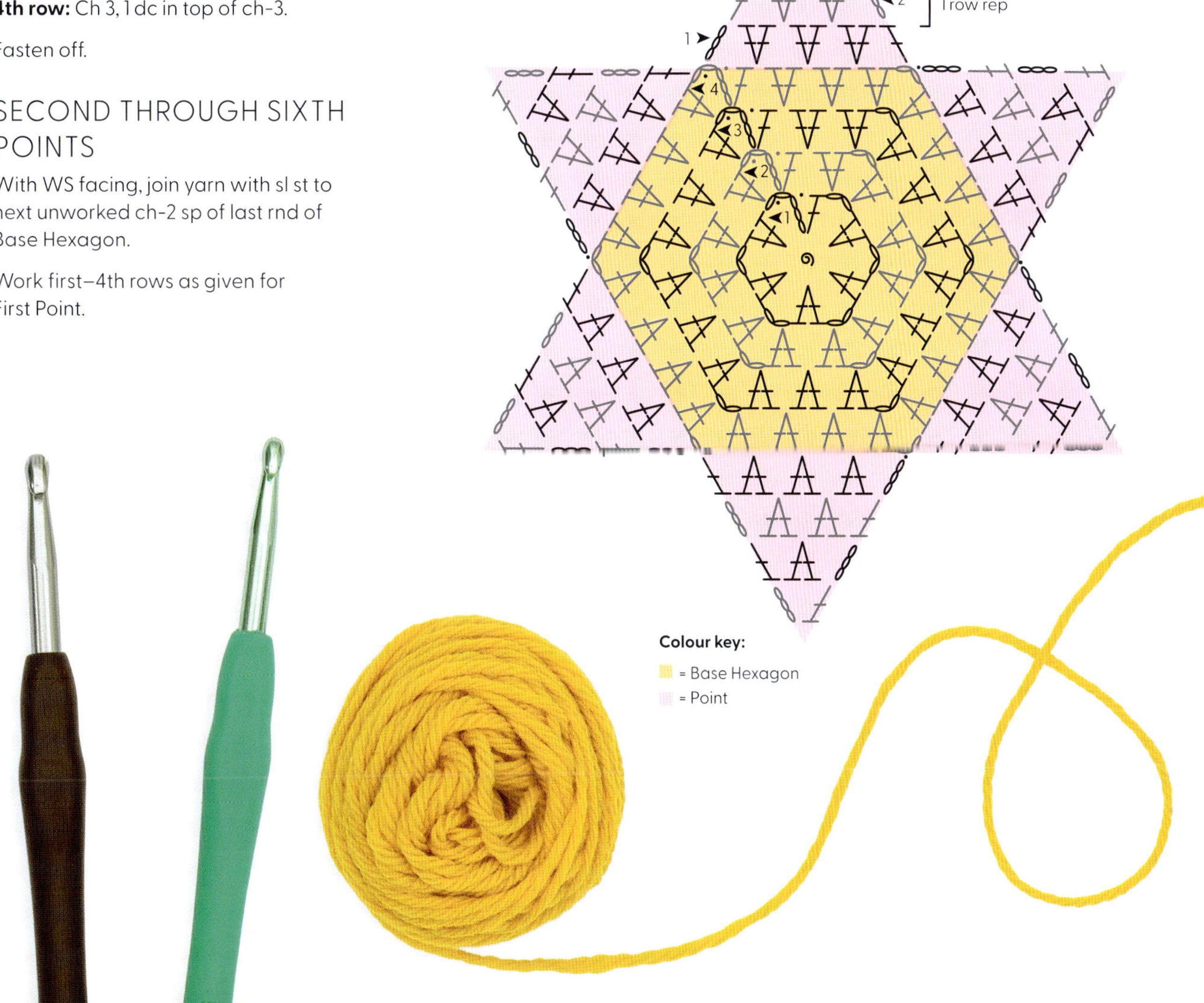

Granny #45

Eight-Point Star

Unlike other granny stars in the galaxy (or at least in this book), this one can be made in continuous rounds. With an easy to memorize three-round repeat you can grow this celestial body to the stars and beyond!

Made in delicate crochet cotton, this star could easily double as a snowflake!

Instructions

Make magic ring.

First rnd: Ch 5 (counts as 1 dc, ch-2 sp throughout), [3 dc, ch 2] 3 times in ring, 2 dc in ring, join with sl st to 3rd ch of beg ch-5.

2nd rnd: Sl st in first ch-2 sp, ch 5, 3 dc in same sp, ch 2, [(3 dc, ch 2) twice in next ch-2 sp] 3 times, 2 dc in first ch-2 sp, join with sl st to 3rd ch of beg ch-5.

3rd rnd: Sl st in first ch-2 sp, ch 5, 3 dc in same sp, [3 dc, ch 2, 3 dc] in each ch-2 sp around, 2 dc in first ch-2 sp, join with sl st to 3rd ch of beg ch-5.

4th rnd: Sl st in first ch-2 sp, ch 5, 3 dc in same sp, ch 1, [3 dc, ch 2, 3 dc, ch 1] in each ch-2 sp around, 2 dc in first ch-2 sp, join with sl st to 3rd ch of beg ch-5.

5th rnd: Sl st in first ch-2 sp, ch 5, 3 dc in same sp, ch 1, 3 dc in next ch-1 sp, ch 1, *[3 dc, ch 2, 3 dc] in next ch-2 sp, ch 1, 3 dc in next ch-1 sp, ch 1; rep from * around, 2 dc in first ch-2 sp, join with sl st to 3rd ch of beg ch-5.

6th rnd: Sl st in first ch-2 sp, ch 5, 3 dc in same sp, ch 1, 3 dc in each of next 2 ch-1 sps, ch 1, *[3 dc, ch 2, 3 dc] in next ch-2 sp, ch 1, 3 dc in each of next 2 ch-1 sps, ch 1; rep from * around, 2 dc in first ch-2 sp, join with sl st to 3rd ch of beg ch-5.

7th rnd: Sl st in first ch-2 sp, ch 5, 3 dc in same sp, ch 1, 3 dc in next ch-1 sp, ch 1, sk next 6 dc (valley), 3 dc in next ch-1 sp, ch 1, *[3 dc, ch 2, 3 dc] in next ch-2 sp, ch 1, 3 dc in next ch-1 sp, ch 1, sk next 6 dc (valley), 3 dc in next ch-1 sp, ch 1; rep from * around, 2 dc in first ch-2 sp, join with sl st to 3rd ch of beg ch-5.

8th rnd: Sl st in first ch-2 sp, ch 5, 3 dc in same sp, ch 1, [3 dc, ch 1] in each ch-1 sp to next ch-2 sp, *[3 dc, ch 2, 3 dc, ch 1] in next ch-2 sp, [3 dc, ch 1] in each ch-1 sp to next ch-2 sp, rep from * around, 2 dc in first ch-2 sp, join with sl st to 3rd ch of beg ch-5.

9th rnd: Sl st in first ch-2 sp, ch 5, 3 dc in same sp, [ch 1, 3 dc in next ch-1 sp] to centre 3-dcCL at valley, [3 dc in next ch-1 sp, ch 1] to next ch-2 sp, *[3 dc, ch 2, 3 dc] in next ch-2 sp, [ch 1, 3 dc in next ch-1 sp] to centre 3-dcCL at valley, [3 dc in next ch-1 sp, ch 1] to next ch-2 sp; rep from * around, 2 dc in first ch-2 sp, join with sl st to 3rd ch of beg ch-5.

10th rnd: Sl st in first ch-2 sp, ch 5, 3 dc in same sp, ch 1, [3 dc, ch 1] in each ch-1 sp to next ch-2 sp (noting 6 dc will be skipped at "valley") *[3 dc, ch 2, 3 dc, ch 1] in next ch-2 sp, [3 dc, ch 1] in each ch-1 sp to next ch-2 sp (noting 6 dc will be skipped at "valley"); rep from * around, 2 dc in first ch-2 sp, join with sl st to 3rd ch of beg ch-5.

To Modify

- Rep 8th–10th rnds to desired size.

The Stats

- Worked in rnds
- Infinite growth potential
- Star shape established in three rnds
- Pairs well with Classic Granny, Equilateral Triangle

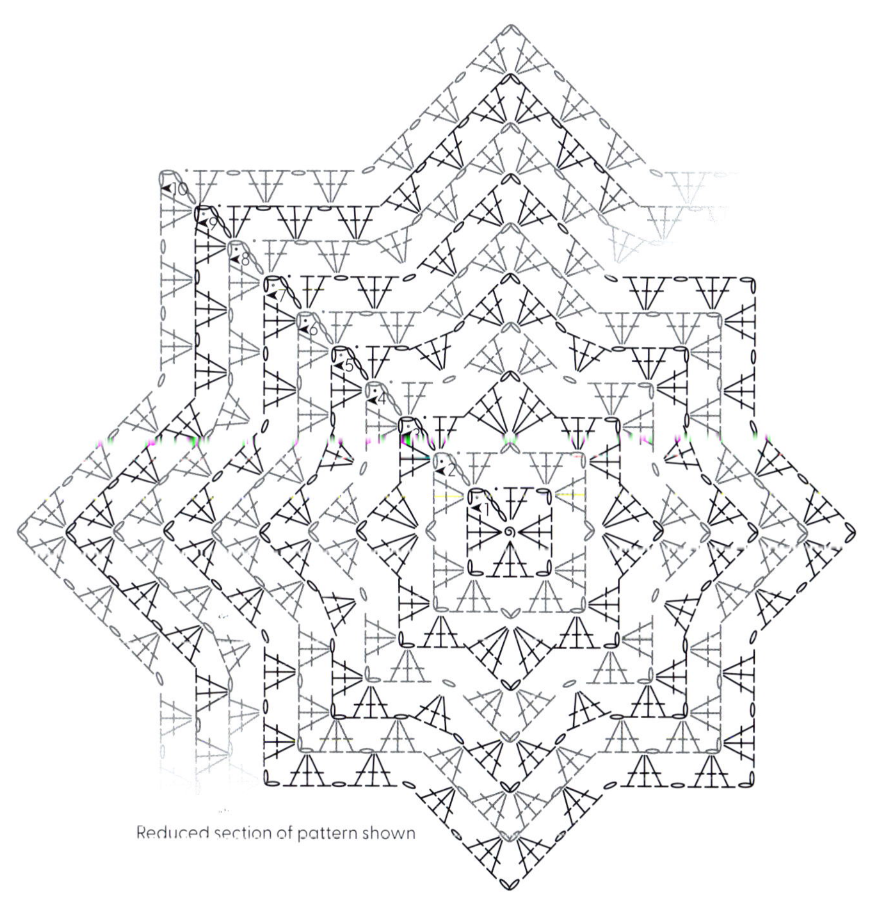

Reduced section of pattern shown

Untangling Rectangling
CALCULATIONS

A granny rectangle can be made to any size you want, but unlike her square compatriot, this granny requires a little bit of forethought. While the round-to-round instructions remain the same no matter what size rectangle you want, the final proportions of your rectangle are dependent on your foundation chain. Determining the number of chains to start with requires a little reverse engineering: DON'T BE SCARED! I've laid out the formula for you, so as long as you can wrangle a calculator you should make out just fine.

STEP 1: DETERMINE YOUR FINISHED MEASUREMENTS

In order to begin this journey, we need to know where you want to end up. What size should the finished rectangle be? For example:

127 x 152.5cm or 50 x 60in

Note: I'm providing examples in both centimetres and inches. I know you're intelligent (you bought this book, after all) so I don't have to tell you to pick one system of measurement and stick with it throughout all the steps, right?

STEP 2: FIND YOUR GAUGE

Swatch and measure your gauge. For these calculations, we'll only be using the stitch (width) gauge over one centimetre or inch. For example:

18 sts ÷ 10cm = 1.8 sts per 1cm or 18 sts ÷ 4in = 4.5 sts per 1in

STEP 3: CALCULATE FINAL NUMBER OF STITCHES AT RECTANGLE SIDES

Grab that calculator! Use your st gauge number to calculate how many sts will be along each side of your rectangle when complete. Final number of side sts = Step 1 x Step 2. For example:

Short rectangle side:

127cm x 1.8 sts per cm = 228.6 sts OR 50in x 4.5 sts per in = 225 sts

Long rectangle side:

152.5cm x 1.8 sts per cm = 274.5 OR 60in x 4.5 sts per in = 270 sts

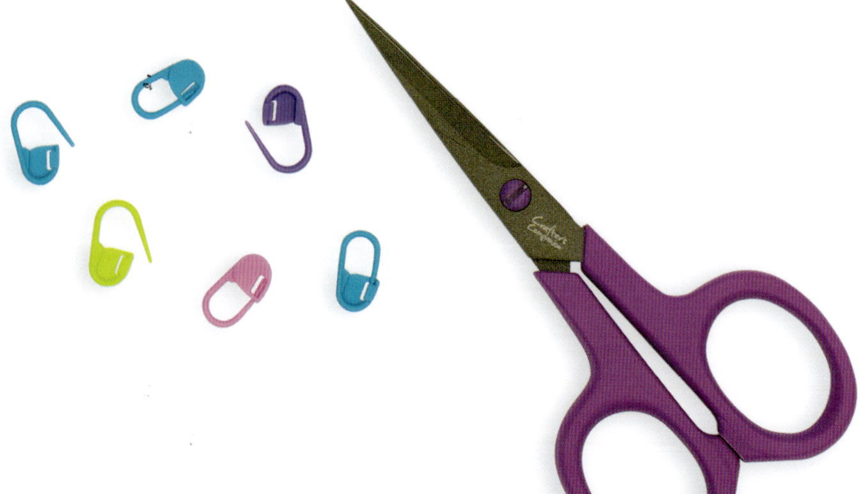

STEP 4: CALCULATE FINAL NUMBER OF PATTERN REPEATS AT SIDES

The classic granny stitch pattern is a multiple of 4: 3 double crochet plus 1 chain space. This means you need to adjust the number of sts in Step 3 to the nearest whole number divisible by 4. For example:

Short rectangle side:

228.6 sts ÷ 4 = 57.15 4, rounded to the nearest whole number= 57

57 reps x 4-st multiple = 228 sts

Long rectangle side:

274.5 sts ÷ 4 = 68.625, rounded to the nearest whole number = 69

69 reps x 4-st multiple = 276 sts

STEP 5: DETERMINE TOTAL NUMBER OF ROUNDS

We now know our final target number of sts for each rectangle side, but what do we start with? If we know how many rnds will be worked, we can find out how many sts will be increased and can use that to reverse-engineer our foundation chain. Luckily, there are key numbers that don't change:

* The short rectangle sides will always have one 4-st pattern rep at the end of the first rnd.
* One 4-st pattern rep is increased each side, each rnd.

So, conveniently, the total number of rnds = number of st reps of the short rectangle side after the last rnd. So:

Total number of rnds = Step 4 for short rectangle side: 57

STEP 6: CALCULATE NUMBER OF STS IN FIRST ROUND OF LONG SIDE

Now use the final number of rnds to determine the number of reps on the long side of the rectangle at the end of the first rnd.

Reps at long side of rectangle at end of first rnd = Step 4 for long rectangle minus Step 5. So:

69 (reps) - 57 (rnds) = 12 reps of 4 sts at end of first rnd: 48 sts

STEP 7: CALCULATE FOUNDATION CHAIN

Almost there! In short, the foundation chain is the number of sts in Step 6 plus 2.

Why 2? If the foundation chain is "Rnd 0", it would be 4 less sts than on the long side of the rectangle at the end of the first rnd.

48 sts end of first rnd minus 4 = 44

But, you need to add chains to account for corner sps and the "turning chain" at the beg of Rnd 1:

+1 as each side is really a multiple of 4 sts + 1 (half of 2-ch corner)

+3 to stand in for first dc of first rnd

+2 for first ch-2 corner sp of first rnd

44 + 1 + 3 + 2 = 50

But instead of subtracting 4 and adding 6, just add 2!

Foundation chain = long side of rectangle after first round + 2, so:

48 + 2 = 50

STEP 8: START RECTANGLING!

Whew! You did it. With your untangled foundation chain, proceed to Basic Rectangle 1! For Basic Rectangle 2, add 5 more chains to the foundation chain.

Note: You'll notice we don't get the same number with metric and imperial calculations. Nothing is wrong, the numbers are just more precise when calculating using a smaller unit of measurement.

Granny #46

Basic Rectangle 1

If you have specific rectangle dimensions in mind, get thee to "Untangling Rectangling". But if you are not a fan of untangling and just want to cut to the crochet already, follow directions here.

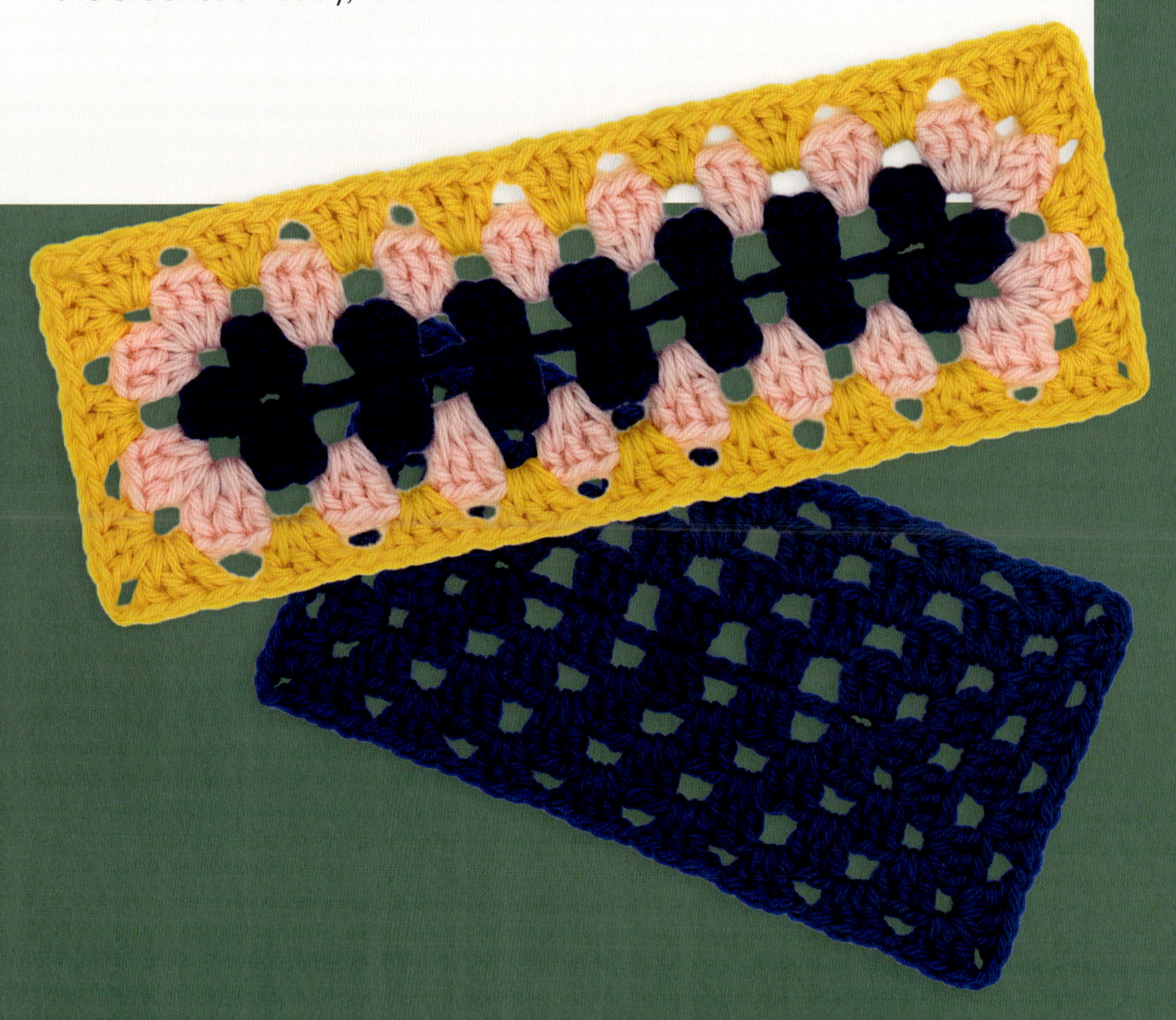

Instructions

Ch 14 (multiple of 4 plus 2, min. of 14).

First rnd: 3 dc in 6th ch from hook (skipped ch-5 counts as 1 dc, ch-2 sp throughout), ch 1, sk next 3 ch, [3 dc, ch 1, sk next 3 ch] to last ch, [3 dc, ch 2, 3 dc, ch 2, 3 dc] in last ch, working across opposite side of foundation chain, ch 1, sk next 3 ch, [3 dc in next ch, ch 1, sk next 3 ch] to last 6 ch, [3 dc, ch 2, 2 dc] in next ch, join with sl st to 3rd ch of beg skipped ch-5.

2nd rnd: Sl st in first ch-2 sp, ch 5, 3 dc in same ch-2 sp, ch 1, [3 dc, ch 1] in each ch-1 sp to next ch-2 sp, [3 dc, ch 2, 3 dc] in next ch-2 sp, ch 1, [3 dc, ch 2, 3 dc] in next ch-2 sp, ch 1, [3 dc, ch 1] in each ch-1 sp to next ch-2 sp, [3 dc, ch 2, 3 dc] in next ch-2 sp, ch 1, 2 dc in first ch-2 sp, join with sl st to 3rd ch of beg ch-5.

3rd rnd: Sl st in first ch-2 sp, ch 5, 3 dc in same ch-2 sp, ch 1, [3 dc, ch 1] in each ch-1 sp to next ch-2 sp, [3 dc, ch 2, 3 dc] in next ch-2 sp, ch 1, 3 dc in next ch-1 sp, ch 1, [3 dc, ch 2, 3 dc] in next ch-2 sp, ch 1, [3 dc, ch 1] in each ch-1 sp to next ch-2 sp, [3 dc, ch 2, 3 dc] in next ch-2 sp, ch 1, 3 dc in next ch-1 sp, ch 1, 2 dc in first ch-2 sp, join with sl st to 3rd ch of beg ch-5.

4th rnd: Sl st in first ch-2 sp, ch 5, 3 dc in same ch-2 sp, ch 1, [3 dc, ch 1] in each ch-1 sp to next ch-2 sp, *[3 dc, ch 2, 3 dc, ch 1] in next ch-2 sp, [3 dc, ch 1] in each ch-1 sp to next ch-2 sp, rep from * twice more, 2 dc in first corner ch-2 sp, join with sl st to 3rd ch of beg ch-5.

To Modify

- Rep 4th rnd to desired size.
- Add or subtract 4 ch to foundation chain to adjust long side of rectangle.

The Stats

- Infinite growth potential
- Worked in rnds
- Pairs well with any square, Half Square Triangle 1 or 2, Trapezoid

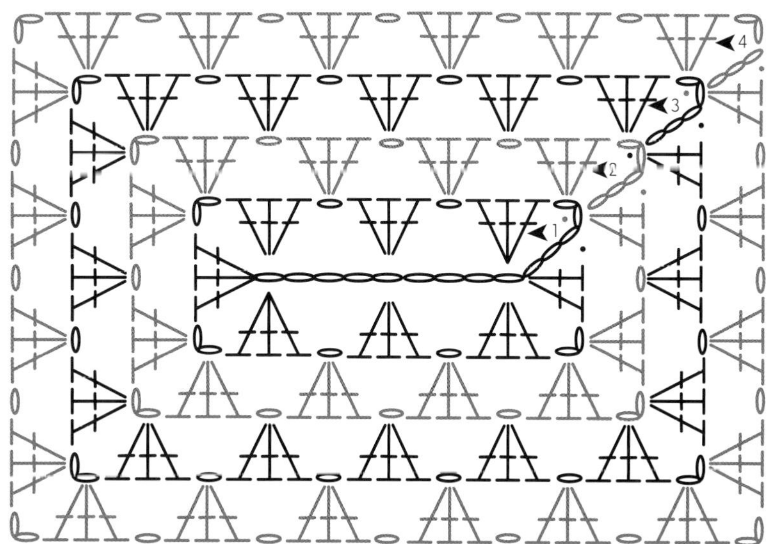

Granny #47

Basic Rectangle 2

This variation of a granny rectangle has you work one row before beginning to work in rounds. The result gives you staggered clusters at the centre of your rectangle instead of the aligned pairs of the Basic Rectangle 1. Swagger and stagger or fine to align? Your choice.

Instructions

Ch 19 (multiple of 4 plus 3, minimum of 15).

First row: 3 dc in 6th ch from hook (skipped ch-5 counts as 1 dc, ch-2 sp), [ch 1, sk next 3 ch, 3 dc in next ch] to last 5 ch, join with sl st to last ch of foundation ch. Do not turn.

Beg working in rnds.

2nd rnd: Sl st in first ch-5 sp, ch 5 (counts as 1 dc, ch-2 sp throughout), [3 dc, ch 2, 3 dc] in same sp, ch 1, working across opposite side of foundation chain, [3 dc in second ch of 3 unworked ch between next two 3-dcCLs of prev row, ch 1] to next ch-5 sp, [(3 dc, ch 2) twice, 3 dc] in next ch-5 sp, [ch 1, 3 dc] in each ch-1 sp around, ch 1, 2 dc in first ch-5 sp, join with sl st to 3rd ch of ch-5.

3rd rnd: Sl st in first ch-5 sp, ch 5, 3 dc in same sp, ch 1, [3 dc, ch 2, 3 dc] in next ch-2 sp, ch 1, [3 dc, ch 1] in each ch-1 sp to next ch-2 sp, [(3 dc, ch 2, 3 dc, ch 1) in next corner ch-2 sp] twice, [3 dc, ch 1] in each ch-1 sp around, 2 dc in first ch-5 sp, join with sl st to 3rd ch of ch-5.

4th rnd: Sl st in first ch-5 sp, ch 5, 3 dc in same sp, ch 1, [3 dc, ch 1] in each ch-1 sp to next ch-2 sp, *[3 dc, ch 2, 3 dc, ch 1] in next ch-2 sp, [3 dc, ch 1] in each ch-1 sp to next ch-2 sp, rep from * to first ch-5 sp, 2 dc in first ch-5 sp, join with sl st to 3rd ch of ch-5.

To Modify

- Repeat 4th rnd to desired size.
- Add or subtract 4 ch to foundation chain to adjust long side of rectangle.

The Stats

- Worked in rnds after First row
- Infinite growth potential
- Pairs well with any square, Half Square Triangle 1 or 2, Parallelogram

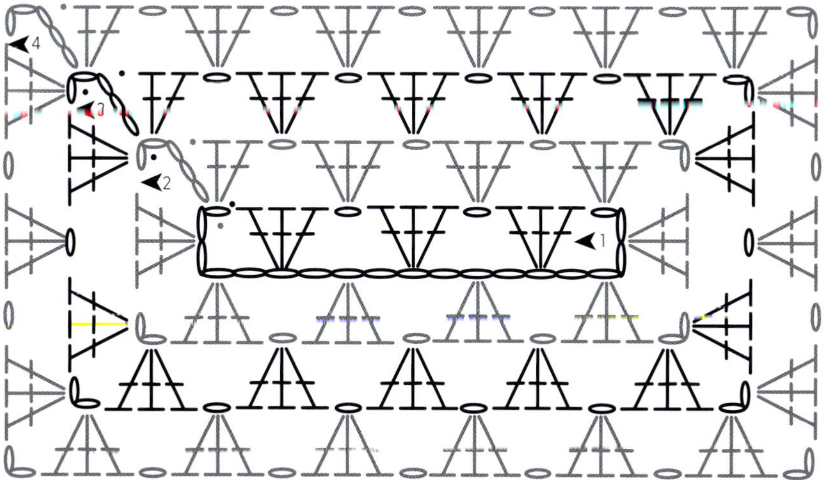

Granny #48

Half Square Rectangle

This variation may find granny in half the shape she used to be, but you can't deny the usefulness of this rectangle. The Classic Granny, the Half Square Triangle and the Half Square Rectangle are great shapes to combine to create simple shaping for garments.

Instructions

Make magic ring.

First row: Ch 3 (counts as 1 dc throughout), [1 dc, ch 2, 3 dc, ch 2, 2 dc] in ring. Turn.

2nd row: Ch 3, [3 dc, ch 2, 3 dc] in next ch-2 sp, ch 1, [3 dc, ch 2, 3 dc] in next ch-2 sp, 1 dc in top of ch-3. Turn.

3rd row: Ch 3, 1 dc in first dc, ch 1, [3 dc, ch 2, 3 dc] in next ch-2 sp, ch 1, 3 dc in next ch-1 sp, ch 1, [3 dc, ch 2, 3 dc] in next ch-2 sp, ch 1, 2 dc in top of ch-3. Turn.

4th row: Ch 3, [3 dc, ch 1] in each ch-1 sp to next ch-2 sp, [3 dc, ch 2, 3 dc] in next ch-2 sp, [ch 1, 3 dc] in each ch-1 sp to next ch-2 sp, ch 1, [3 dc, ch 2, 3 dc] in next ch-2 sp, [ch 1, 3 dc] in each ch-1 sp to end of row, 1 dc in top of ch-3. Turn.

5th row: Ch 3, 1 dc in first dc, ch 1, [3 dc, ch 1] in each ch-1 sp to next ch-2 sp, [3 dc, ch 2, 3 dc] in next ch-2 sp, [ch 1, 3 dc] in each ch-1 sp to next ch-2 sp, ch 1, [3 dc, ch 2, 3 dc] in next ch-2 sp, [ch 1, 3 dc] in each ch-1 sp to end of row, ch 1, 2 dc in top of ch-3. Turn.

To Modify

- Rep 4th and 5th rows to desired size.

The Stats

- Worked in rows
- Infinite growth potential
- Pairs well with any square or rectangle, Half Square Triangle 1 or 2

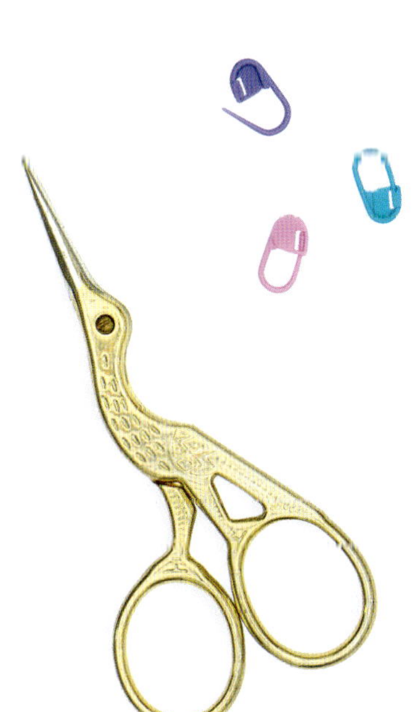

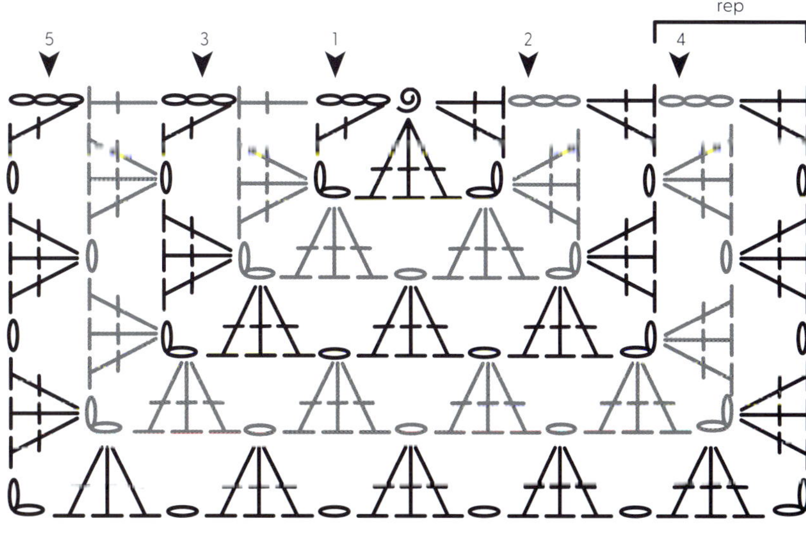

Parallelogram

Technically, all rectangles are parallelograms, but this long, leaning shape (a rectangle in a windstorm!) is the one I think of when I hear the term. It fits well with triangles and squares to create interesting patterns. As an added bonus, you can easily create zig-zag shapes by switching up the direction of the lean.

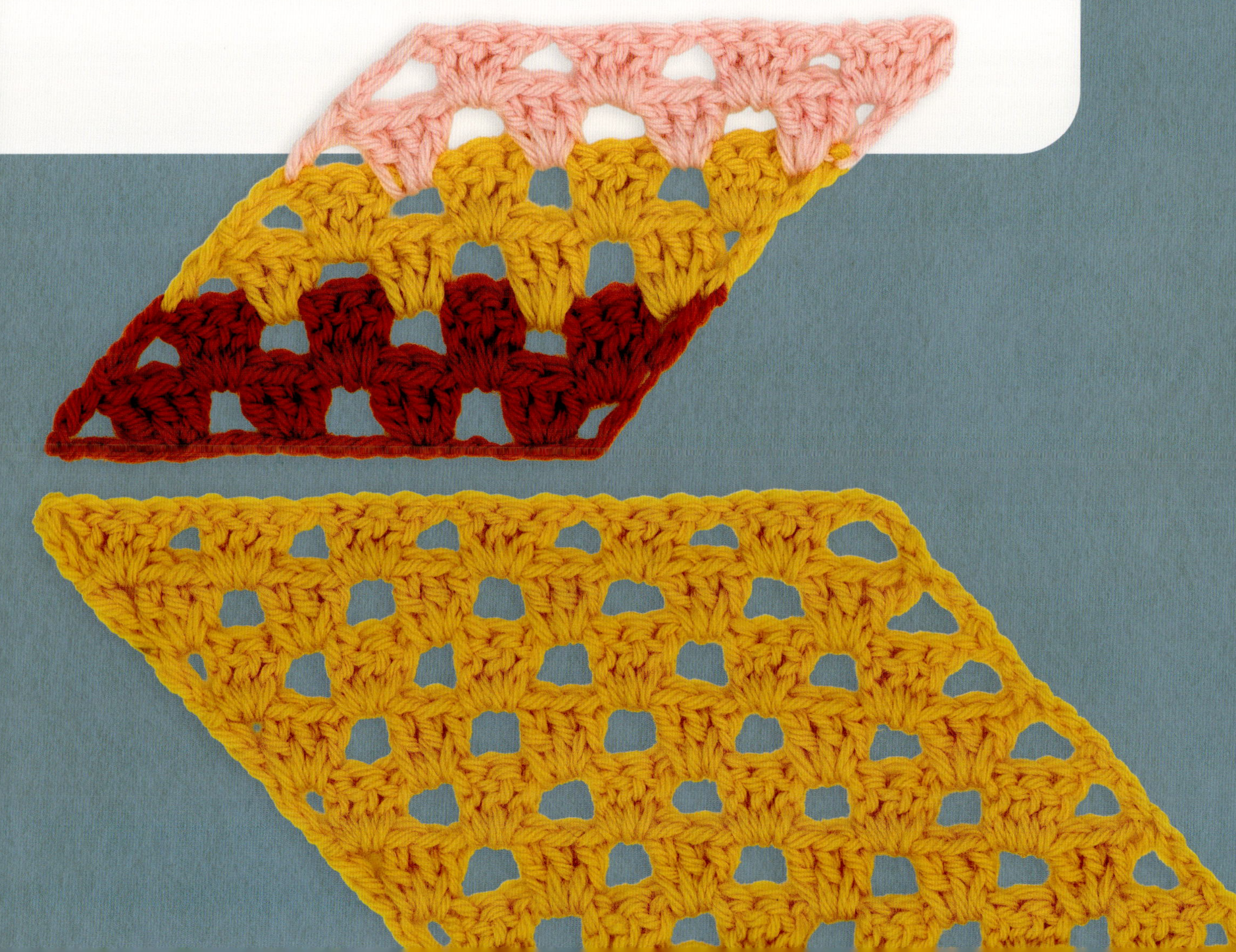

Instructions

RIGHT-LEANING

Ch 21 (multiple of 4 plus 1, minimum of 13).

First row: 3 dc in 5th ch from hook (skipped ch-4 counts as 1 dc, ch-1 sp), [ch 1, sk next 3 ch, 3 dc in next ch] to last 4 ch, sk next 3 ch, 1 dc in last ch. Turn.

2nd row: Ch 3 (counts as 1 dc), [3 dc, ch 1] in each ch-1 sp to last ch-4 sp, 3 dc in last ch-4 sp, ch 1, 1 dc in 3rd ch of ch-4. Turn.

3rd row: Ch 4 (counts as 1 dc, ch-1 sp), 3 dc in first ch-1 sp, [ch 1, 3 dc] in each ch-1 sp to last 4 sts, sk next 3 dc, 1 dc in top of ch-3. Turn.

LEFT-LEANING

Ch 20 (multiple of 4, minimum of 12).

First row: 3 dc in 7th ch from hook (skipped ch-6 counts as 1 dc, skipped ch-3), [ch-1, sk next 3 ch, 3 dc in next ch] to last ch, ch 1, 1 dc in last ch. Turn.

2nd row: Ch 4 (counts as 1 dc, ch-1 sp), 3 dc in first ch-1 sp, [ch 1, 3 dc] in each ch-1 sp to last 4 sts, sk next 3 dc, 1 dc in top of ch-3. Turn.

3rd row: Ch 3 (counts as 1 dc), [3 dc, ch 1] in each ch-1 sp to last ch-4 sp, 3 dc in last ch-4 sp, ch 1, 1 dc in 3rd ch of ch-4. Turn.

To Modify (both versions)

- Rep 2nd and 3rd rows to desired length.
- Add or subtract 4 ch to foundation chain to adjust width.
- Alternate several left-leaning and right-leaning rows to make yourself a zig-zag!

The Stats

- Worked in rows
- Infinite growth potential
- Can lean left or right

RIGHT-LEANING

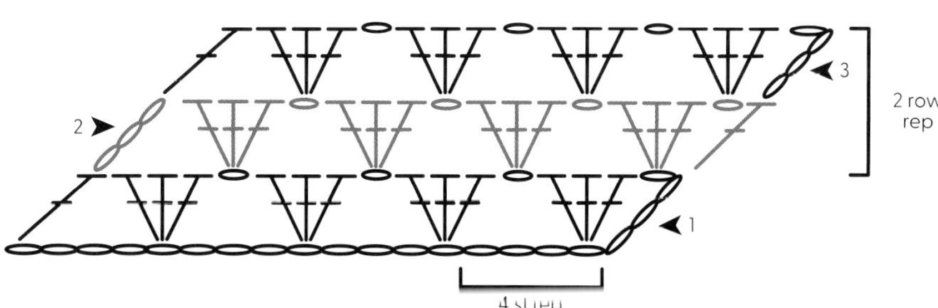

LEFT-LEANING

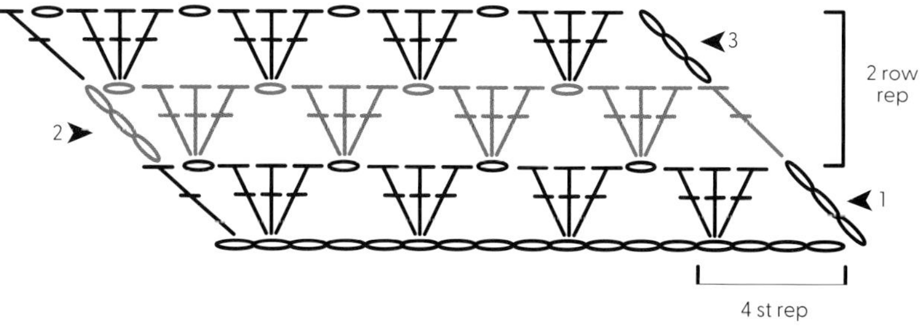

Granny #50

Mitred Corner Rectangle

Mitred squares can be combined in all sorts of ways to create fun, geometric patterns, so why not stretch the limits and try out a mitred rectangle? Use multiple colours for maximum impact and the mightiest mitre!

Instructions

Ch 12 (multiple of 4, minimum of 12).

First row: 1 dc in 4th ch from hook (skipped ch-3 counts as 1 dc), *ch 1, sk next 3 ch, 3 dc in next ch; rep from * to last 4 ch, ch 1, sk next 3 ch, [3 dc, ch 2, 2 dc] in last ch. Turn.

2nd row: Ch 3 (counts as 1 dc throughout), [3 dc, ch 2, 3 dc] in next ch-2 sp, [ch 1, 3 dc] in each ch-1 sp to last 2 sts, 1 dc in top of ch-3. Turn.

3rd row: Ch 3, 1 dc in first dc, ch 1, [3 dc, ch 1] in each ch-1 sp to next ch-2 sp, [3 dc, ch 2, 3 dc] in next ch-2 sp, ch 1, 2 dc in top of ch-3. Turn.

4th row: Ch 3, [3 dc, ch 1] in each ch-1 sp to next ch-2 sp, [3 dc, ch 2, 3 dc] in next ch-2 sp, [ch 1, 3 dc] in each ch-1 sp to last 2 sts, 1 dc in top of ch-3. Turn.

5th row: Ch 3, 1 dc in first dc, ch 1, [3 dc, ch 1] in each ch-1 sp to next ch-2 sp, [3 dc, ch 2, 3 dc] in next ch-2 sp, [ch 1, 3 dc] in each ch-1 sp to last 4 sts, ch 1, 2 dc in top of ch-3. Turn.

To Modify

- Rep 4th and 5th rows to desired size.
- Add or subtract 4 ch to foundation chain to adjust long rectangle side.

The Stats

- Worked in rows
- Infinite growth potential
- Pairs well with Mitred Square, all other squares, all rectangles

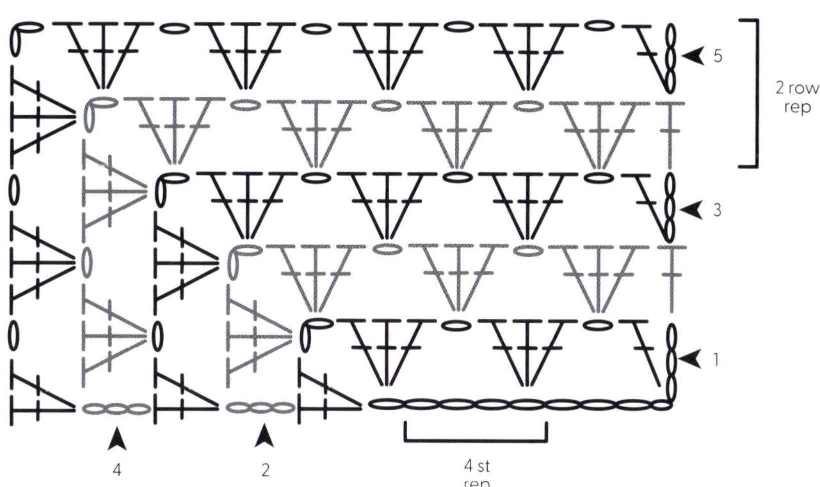

The
Finishing

Rock the Block

BLOCKING

WET BLOCKING

Wet blocking requires completely soaking your crochet piece, so allow time for your work to air-dry. Animal fibres like 100% wool or alpaca will felt or "full" with water, heat and agitation, so make sure to use cool water and gentle handling when wet blocking these fibres.

1. Fill a bowl or sink with lukewarm water and add a dash of wool wash/ no rinse wash if desired (I like Eucalan or Soak).
2. Add your crochet piece(s), ensuring they are fully immersed.
3. Allow your work to soak for long enough that the fabric is fully saturated. This varies but 10–30 minutes is a good ballpark.
4. Remove your work from its bath and gently squeeze out most of the water.
5. Optional: Lay your work on a towel, then roll it up. Press firmly (or dance on) the towel-roll. This technique really gets out most of the water and will speed up your dry-time.
6. Pin your piece to the desired measurements and allow to air-dry completely before unpinning.

STEAM BLOCKING

Steam blocking is a nice speedy blocking method and only requires a conventional iron with a steam setting. If you have a garment steamer: bonus! Wool and cotton can handle the heat, but be careful with synthetics that could melt: make sure your iron surface doesn't actually touch your work. Don't forget to make sure your blocking surface can also handle high heat.

1. Heat your iron to the highest setting with full steam (or fire up that garment steamer).
2. Pin your dry piece(s) to the desired measurements.
3. Holding your iron a few inches above your work, shoot your piece with a few blasts of steam. If using a garment steamer, hover the nozzle across the piece. Do not touch the surface of the iron or steamer to your work. The idea is to have the steam penetrate your piece, but not to press or iron it.
4. If needed, manipulate and re-pin your pieces as needed while they are still warm and damp.
5. Allow your work to completely dry and cool before unpinning.

SPRAY BLOCKING

This is the method to use if you are using delicate fibres or unsure of the fibre content of your yarn. Fibres like cashmere, silk and fine-weight, single-ply yarns are vulnerable to breakage when wet, so pinning and shaping while the yarn is dry is your safest bet.

1. Pin your dry piece(s) to the desired measurements.
2. Fill a clean spray bottle with water (cold is fine).
3. Give your work a good spray until quite damp.
4. Allow your work to completely dry and cool before unpinning.

Good to know:

Commercially made blocking mats and boards are widely available but any large flat surface that is water-resistant and that you are able to stick a pin in will work.

BLOCKING MULTIPLE MOTIFS

If working a patchwork project, you may have dozens of squares or shapes that all need to be the same size. It's a lot easier to block a small square than a whole afghan, so I advise blocking all the pieces before assembly.

Tips for blocking multiple crochet pieces of the same shape and size:

- Line 'em up! Aligning the sides of squares or other straight-sided shapes side-by-side means you can check measurements all at once. If your blocking surface has a grid you're ahead of the game.
- Stack 'em up! Placing several pieces on top of each other means you can measure and align all edges and even use less pins. The downside is a longer dry-time.
- Divide 'em up! A big patchwork project might have dozens of motifs to block. For your sanity, block them in batches. Bonus, use your first batch pieces as templates when blocking the rest.

Before blocking

After blocking

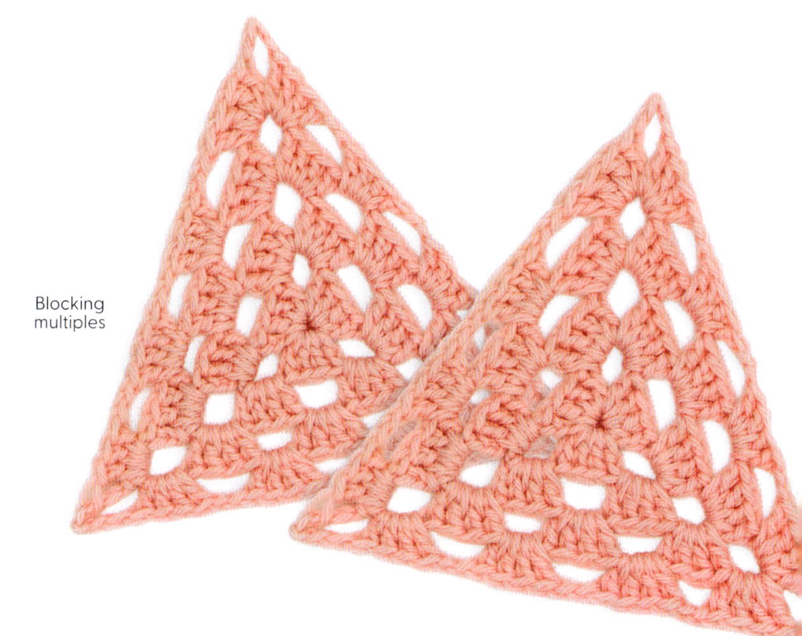

Blocking multiples

	Wet Blocking	Steam Blocking	Spray Blocking
Approx time commitment	24 hrs +	30 mins	12 hrs +
Results	Great	Good	Good
Best used for	Natural fibres	Natural fibres, lightweight yarns	Delicate and unknown fibres, lightweight yarns
Not great for	Delicate fibres	Synthetics	Thick yarns

All Together Now
SEAMING

MATTRESS STITCH SEAM

Pros:

- ✱ Invisible on the right side
- ✱ Strong seam

Cons:

- ✱ Time consuming

This seam may go by other names, but I call it mattress stitch because it is similar to the seam of the same name in knitting. This seam works best when joining tops of stitches to tops of stitches, which will be the case with any crochet piece worked in rounds from the centre-out. When worked through back loops only as outlined here, it's virtually invisible on the right side of the work, making it an ideal choice for joining pieces of different colours.

1. Place the crochet pieces on a flat surface with the RIGHT SIDES facing up and the edges to be joined aligned.
2. Thread a yarn needle with matching yarn. Bring the needle through the back loop only of the first stitch on the first crochet piece from back (WS) to front (RS). Draw the yarn through leaving a tail for weaving in after seaming is complete.
3. Bring the needle through the back loop only of the first stitch on the second crochet piece from front (RS) to back (WS).
4. Working into the back loops only of the first piece, bring the needle through the previously worked stitch from front (RS) to back (WS), then up from back (WS) to front (RS) through the next stitch. Draw the yarn through loosely.
5. Working into the back loops only of the second piece, bring the needle through the previously worked stitch from front (RS) to back (WS), then up from back (WS) to front (RS) through the next stitch. Draw the yarn through loosely.
6. Repeat Steps 4 and 5 until all stitches have been worked.
7. Pull both ends of the seaming yarn to adjust the seam to the desired tightness, and weave in ends.

WHIPSTITCH SEAM

This quick and easy seam looks the same on both sides of your work, making it a good choice for reversible projects. The downside is that, well, it's visible, so use a matching colour to sew your seam if you don't want it to show.

1. Hold two squares together, aligning the edges to be seamed (with either right side or wrong side facing each other).
2. Thread a yarn needle with matching yarn and insert the needle through both loops or next space of the first stitch on the first piece, then both loops of the corresponding stitch or space on the second piece.
3. Draw the yarn through the stitches leaving a tail for weaving in when seaming is complete.
4. Inserting the needle in the same direction as previously, take it through both loops of the next stitch on the first piece, then through both loops of the corresponding stitch on the second piece.
5. Repeat Step 4 until all stitches have been worked.
6. Cut the yarn and weave in ends.

SLIP STITCH SEAM 1: WRONG SIDE

Worked with a crochet hook instead of a needle and thread, many crocheters love a slip stitch for a quick and easy seam. Bonus: if you make a mistake, you can pull out this seam with a simple tug rather than unpick each stitch. This version is worked on the wrong side through back loops only, which creates a ridge on the wrong side but is virtually invisible on the right side.

1. Hold the two crochet pieces with right sides together and edges to be seamed aligned.
2. Join the yarn by inserting the hook through the back loop only of the first stitch on each crochet piece, drawing up a loop. Note the back loops will be the exterior loops when the pieces are sandwiched together.
3. Working through both thicknesses, sl st in the back loops only of each stitch to the end of the seam.
4. Fasten off and weave in ends.

SLIP STITCH SEAM 2: RIGHT SIDE

This seam has all the same benefits as the Slip Stitch Seam 1, with the added bonus of lying flat. It will create a visible chain between your seamed pieces that you can use for decorative effect in a contrast yarn, or stay matchy-matchy for a more subtle look.

1. Place the crochet pieces on a flat surface with the RIGHT SIDES facing up and the edges to be joined aligned.
2. Join the yarn by inserting the hook through the back loop only of the first stitch on one crochet piece and then the other, drawing up a loop.
3. Keeping the working yarn at the WS and working through both thicknesses, sl st in the back loops only of each stitch to the end of the seam. In this method, the back loops of one piece will be stacked on top of the back loops of the second piece as they are joined. Begin each sl st on the same piece to allow for this to happen.
4. Fasten off and weave in ends.

BACKSTITCH SEAM

This seam is great for sewing appliqués because it creates a neat line of stitches on the right side of the work. Backstitch can also be used to sew strong garment or other project seams, but it leaves a significant ridge on the wrong side, so it isn't ideal for joining pieces that need to lie flat next to each other.

1. Hold two crochet pieces with right sides together and edges to be seamed aligned. OR, if sewing an appliqué, pin it to the base piece and work with the right side facing.
2. Thread the needle with yarn and insert it from back to front through both thicknesses into the second stitch or space to be worked. Draw the yarn through, leaving a tail for weaving in when seaming is complete.
3. Working backward, insert the needle from front to back through the first stitch or space to be worked and draw the yarn through.
4. Working forward, insert the needle from back to front through the next stitch or space and draw the yarn through.
5. Working backward, insert the needle from front to back through the same stitch or space where the previous stitch began.
6. Repeat Steps 4 and 5 until the seam is complete, cut the yarn and weave in ends.

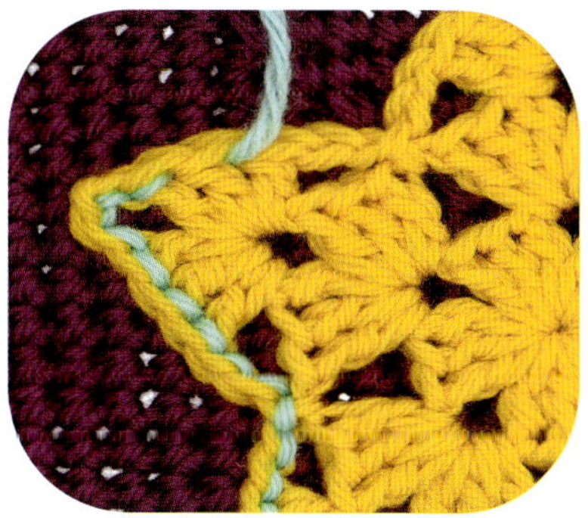

JOIN AS YOU GO (J.A.Y.GO)

Hate seaming? This method of joining is game-changing! Strategic slip stitches join your squares as you crochet the last round and before you know it, you're done.

The instructions given here are for joining four squares while simultaneously working their last rounds. Once you know the basics, you can easily adapt the technique to join more squares, or other shapes.

Note

* Best for joining squares where the last round of each square is the same colour.
* When slip stitching into finished squares, always insert the hook from front to back (top to bottom) into the chain space for best results.
* Orientation directions (bottom-left, etc) refer to orientation of the work when it is completed (and matches the stitch diagram). Squares will need to be turned in different directions as you work.
* Instructions as written require the squares to have at least two rounds completed before joining.
* Colours in the stitch diagram and photo correspond with each step of the instructional text.

Continuous J.A.Y.Go Join

Begin with four squares with all but the final round completed. Work with the right side of the squares facing at all times and do not break yarn or change colours between steps. Colour changes shown in photo are to differentiate between steps.

1. **Work right, top and left side of Square 1 (shown in purple):** Join yarn with a sl st to bottom right corner ch-2 sp of Square 1. Ch 5 and work in granny pattern (as outlined in Classic Granny Version 1) across the right, top and left side ending with [3 dc, ch 2] in bottom-left corner ch-2 sp.
2. **Join unfinished right side of Square 2 to the left side of Square 1 (shown in blue):** 3 dc in bottom-right corner ch-2 sp of Square 2, sl st in next ch-1 sp up left side of Square 1, *3 dc in next ch-1 sp of right side of Square 2, sl st in next ch-1 sp up left side of Square 1; rep from * to corner ch-2 sps, 3 dc in corner ch-2 sp of Square 2, ch 1, sl st in corner ch-2 sp of Square 1, ch 1, continue around Square 2 only, completing top edge in granny pattern ending with [3 dc, ch 2] in top-left corner ch-2 sp.
3. **Join unfinished bottom side of Square 3 to top side of Square 2 (shown in orange):** 3 dc in bottom-left corner ch-2 sp of Square 3, sl st in next ch-1 sp of top side of Square 2, *3 dc in next ch-1 sp of bottom side of Square 3, sl st in next ch-1 sp of top side of Square 2; rep from * to corner ch-2 sps, 3 dc in corner ch-2 sp of Square 3, ch 1, sl st in corner ch-2 sp of Square 1 (noting you are joining diagonally), ch 1, continue around Square 3 only, completing right side edge in granny pattern ending with [3 dc, ch 2] in top-right corner ch-2 sp.
4. **Join unfinished left side of Square 4 to right side of Square 3 (shown in green):** 3 dc in top-left corner ch-2 sp of Square 4, sl st in next ch-1 sp of right side of Square 3, *3 dc in next ch-1 sp of right side of Square 4, sl st in next ch-1 sp of right side of Square 3; rep from * to corner ch-2 sps, ch 1, 3 dc in corner ch-2 sp of Square 4, ch 1, sl st in corner ch-2 sp of Square 2 (noting you are joining diagonally), ch 1.
5. **Join unfinished bottom side of Square 4 to top side of Square 1 (shown in teal):** 3 dc in same corner ch-2 sp of Square 4, sl st in next ch-1 sp of top side of Square 1, *3 dc in next ch-1 sp of bottom side of Square 4, sl st in next ch-1 sp of top side of Square 1; rep from * to corner ch-2 sps, 3 dc in corner ch-2 sp of Square 4, ch 1, sl st in corner ch-2 sp of Square 1, ch 1.
6. **Complete unfinished remaining edges of all squares (shown in red):** continue in granny stitch pattern around rem unfinished edges of Squares 4, 3, 2 and 1 working [ch 1, sl st in ch-2 sp, ch 1] at each ch-2 sp between squares, join with sl st to 3rd ch of beg ch-5. Fasten off.

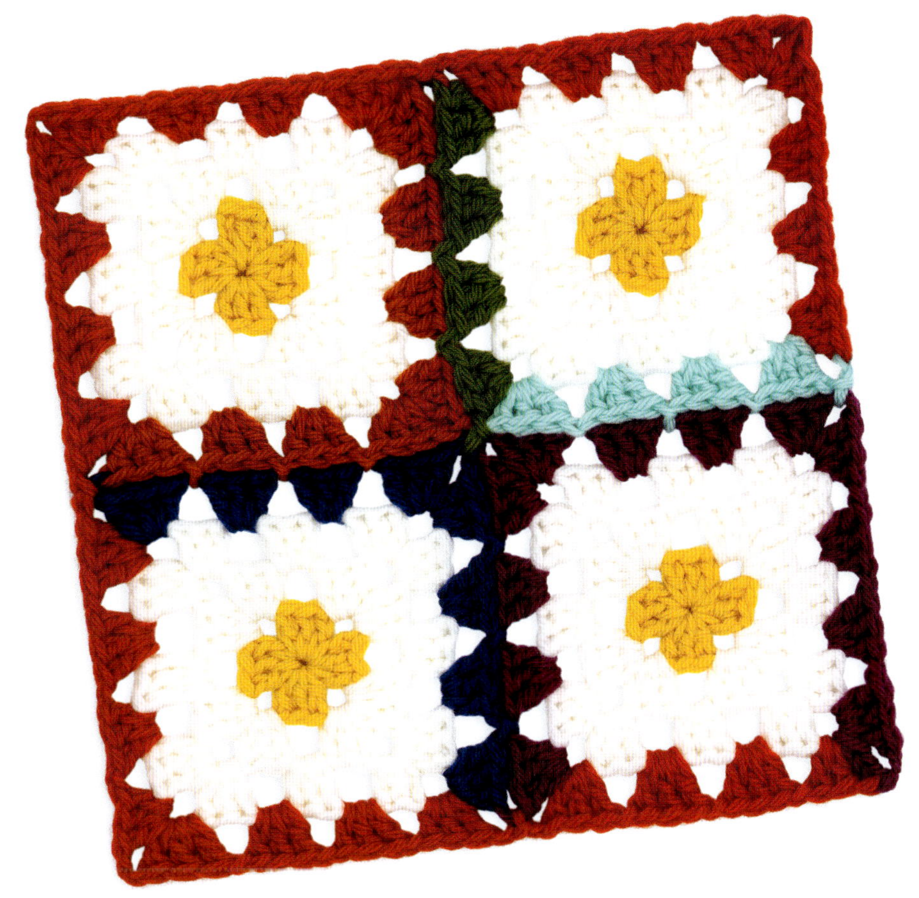

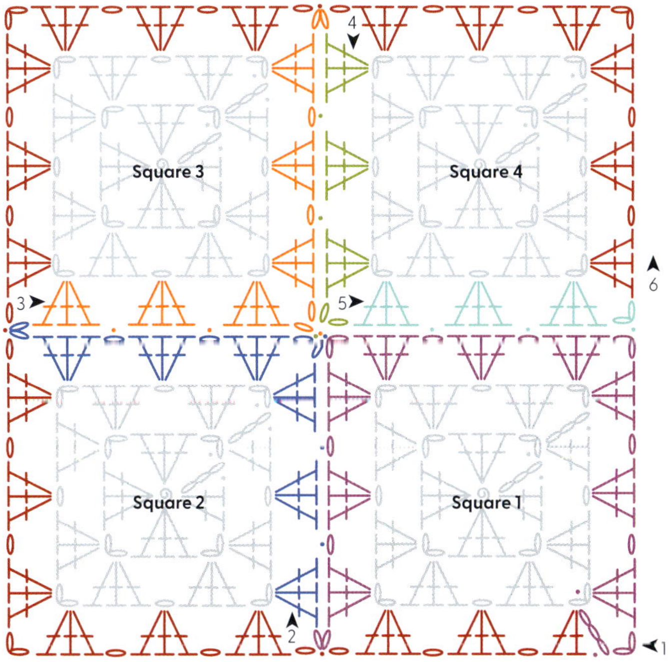
Square 3
Square 4
Square 2
Square 1
1
2
3
4
5
6

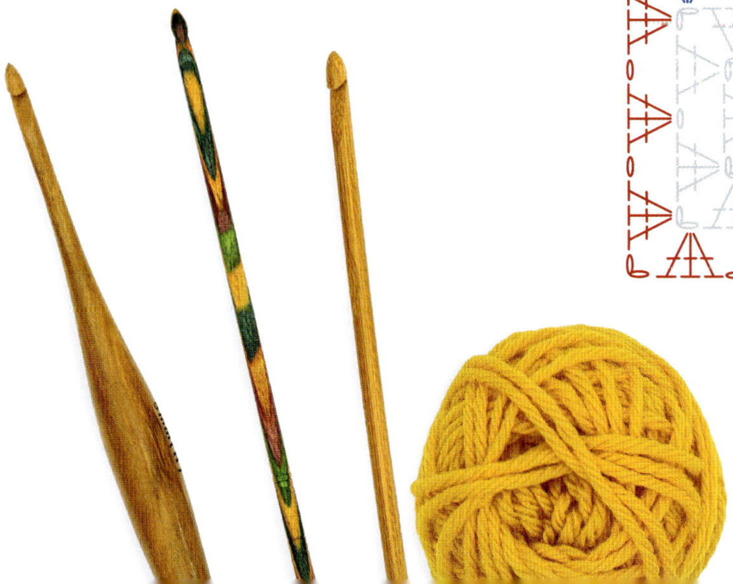

Living on the Edge
BORDERS

SINGLE CROCHET BORDER

One or two rounds of single crochet makes a nice clean border to any project. A single crochet edge can also be a great way to prep shapes for seaming.

Instructions

With right side facing, join yarn with a sl st to top right corner st or sp of work.

In rows – First row: Ch 1 (does not count as st), sc in each st or sp to end of row. Turn.

Rep this row as many times as desired.

In the rnd – First rnd: Ch 1 (does not count as st), 2 sc in first st, sc in each st or sp around, working 3 sc in each 90° corner, 1 sc in same sp as first 2 sc, join with sl st to first sc.

Rep this rnd as many times as desired.

Note

Instructions are written for working into a square or rectangle, or shapes that have been joined to form a square or rectangle. Modifications for other shapes are noted where possible.

MODIFICATIONS FOR OTHER SHAPES

As single crochet stitches are short, you can usually get away working one stitch in each stitch around a curved shape without adding increases if you're only working one row/round. If adding multiple rows or rounds of single crochet, use these general guidelines:

Exterior corners: Work 3 sc in the corner space for a 90° corner, 2 sc for a lesser angle, 4 sc or more for a sharper angle.

Interior corner: Work sc2tog (across 1 st before and 1 st after corner) for a 90° corner. For sharper interior angles you can try one or more sc2tog before and after the turn.

Exterior curve: Work evenly spaced increases (2 sc in the same sp). The sharper the curve, the more increases needed.

Interior curve: Work evenly spaced decreases (sc2tog). The sharper the curve the more decreases needed.

REVERSE SINGLE CROCHET BORDER

Reverse single crochet (aka crab stitch) is a magical technique where simply working the standard single crochet stitch in the opposite direction creates a cool, corded-look edge. For right-handed crocheters, this usually means working left-to-right instead of right-to left: for lefties: the opposite. While the technique will work on any edge, I personally prefer working a row/rnd of standard single crochet prior to the reverse single crochet row/rnd.

Note

- Due to the twisted nature of this stitch, it is best used as the final row or round as you really can't work into the top of these stitches.
- Unlike the single crochet border, I find there's no need to work extra stitches to turn a corner though the result is a slightly softer corner.

Instructions

With right side facing join yarn with a sl st to desired st or sp.

In rows/in the rnd: Ch 1 (does not count as st), working in the opposite direction than usual, reverse sc in each st or sp to end of row or rnd. If working in the rnd: Join with sl st in first sc.

DOUBLE CROCHET BORDER

For a more substantial border than single crochet; double it!

Instructions

With right side facing join yarn with a sl st to top-right corner of work.

In rows: Ch 3 (counts as 1 dc), 1 dc in each st or sp to end of row. Turn.

Rep this row as many times as desired.

In the rnd: Ch 3 (counts as 1 dc), 2 dc in same sp as sl st, 1 dc in each st or sp around, working 5 dc in each corner, 2 dc in same sp as first 3 dc, join with sl st in top of beg ch-3.

Rep this rnd as many times as desired.

> **Note**
>
> If working a border across a row of joined granny squares, work only one single or double crochet stitch in each corner space of the squares along the edges.

GRANNY BORDER

Why not keep things all-granny-all-the-time?

Granny stitch border across a row of joined Classic Granny squares

Join yarn with sl st to top-right corner ch-2 sp.

First row: Ch 3 (counts as 1 dc throughout), 1 dc in same sp as sl st, ch 1, [3 dc, ch 1] in each ch-1 sp to next ch-2 sp, *1 dc in next ch-2 sp, dc2tog drawing up first st in same ch-2 sp and 2nd st in next ch-2 sp, 1 dc in same ch-2 sp, ch 1, [3 dc, ch 1] in each ch-1 sp to next ch-2 sp; rep from * to last ch-2 sp, 2 dc in last ch-2 sp. Turn.

2nd row: Ch 3, 3 dc in next ch-1 sp, [ch 1, 3 dc] in each ch-1 sp to last 2 sts, 1 dc in top of ch-3. Turn.

3rd row: Ch 3, 1 dc in first dc, ch 1, [3 dc, ch 1] in each ch-1 sp to end of row, 2 dc in top of beg ch-3. Turn.

Rep 2nd and 3rd rows desired number of times.

Granny stitch border around joined Classic Granny squares

With RS facing join yarn with sl st to any exterior corner ch-2 sp.

First round: Ch 5 (counts as 1 dc, ch-2 sp), 2 dc in same sp, *ch 1, [1 dc, ch 1] in each ch-1 sp to next ch-2 corner sp **, [1 dc in ch-2 corner sp, dc2tog drawing up first st in same ch-2 corner sp and 2nd st in next corner ch-2 sp, 1 dc in same sp, ch 1, (1 dc, ch 1) in each ch-1 sp to next ch-2 corner sp] rep to exterior corner ch-2 sp [2 dc, ch 2, 2 dc] in corner ch-2 sp; rep from * twice more, then from * to ** once, 2 dc in first exterior corner ch-2 sp, join with sl st in top of beg ch-3.

2nd and subsequent rnds: Work in granny stitch as given for the Classic Granny Version 1.

MODIFICATIONS

To work a granny border across/around a different stitch pattern, each side you are working into must have a multiple of 4 plus 1 sts.

Single Crochet | Reverse Single Crochet | Double Crochet | Granny Border

The Sampler

What do you get when you mix 15 different granny shapes, two seaming techniques and three borders? A darn fine sampler blanket! Make as I've outlined here, OR mix and match sections to create your own unique design.

Materials

Cascade 220 Superwash (100% Superwash Wool), DK/light worsted weight; 200m/220yd per 100g/3½oz ball

- A: 836 Pink Ice – 2 balls or 345m/377yd
- B: 809 Really Red – 1 ball or 155m/170yd
- C: 823 Burnt Orange – 2 balls or 185m/202yd
- D: 346 Daisy Yellow – 2 balls or 280m/306yd
- E: 802 Green Apple – 2 balls or 265m/290yd
- F: 1973 Seafoam Heather – 2 balls or 310m/339yd
- G: 813 Blue Velvet – 1 ball or 195m/213yd
- H: 815 Black – 3 balls or 540m/591yd
- I: 871 White – 2 balls or 375m/410yd

Size 5mm (US size H-8) crochet hook or size needed to obtain gauge.

Gauge

14 sts x 10 rows = 10cm (4in) in granny stitch pattern.

5 rnd Classic Granny square = 15cm (6in).

Finished Measurements

Approx. 127 x 168cm (50 x 66in).

DIRECTIONS

Each section is outlined in diagram and is composed of one or more shapes from The Shapes section of this book. Reference the appropriate page for specific instructions for each shape. Note that sections 1–5 and 7–10 are used twice and section 6 is used four times in the layout and the number of shapes in these sections refers to the total number required for the blanket.

SECTION 1

Finished measurements: 30.5 x 30.5cm (12 x 12in)

- Make 2 in F – Classic Granny (any version): 5 rnds.
- Make 2 in E – Half Square Triangle 1: 5 rows.
- Make 4 in F – Half Square Triangle 1: 3 rows.
- Make 4 in C – Parallelogram as follows: With foundation chain of 25, work 5 right-leaning rows, fasten off. Rotate work 180°. Working across opposite side of foundation chain, work 5 left-leaning rows.

SECTION 2

Finished measurements: 30.5 x 30.5cm (12 x 12in)

- Make 2 – Diamond in a Square: 4-rnd Base Square in I, Triangles in H, 4 plain rnds in D.

SECTION 3

Finished measurements: 30.5 x 30.5cm (12 x 12in)

- Make 2 – Octagon: 10 rnds, alternating rnds of A and E, beg with A.
- With E, work four "Points" as given in Any-Size Five-Point Star, joining yarn at every second side to create a square.

SECTION 4

Finished measurements: 30.5 x 30.5cm (12 x 12in)

- Make 2 in D – Classic Granny (any version): 6 rnds.
- Make 2 in F – Parallelogram (Left-Leaning): Foundation ch of 29, 9 rows.
- Make 2 in B – Parallelogram (Right-Leaning): Foundation ch of 28, 9 rows.
- Make 4 in G – Half Square Triangle 1: 4 rows .

SECTION 5

Finished measurements: 30.5 x 30.5cm (12 x 12in)

- Make 2 – Quad Colour Square: 5 rnds with B as A, D as B, E as C and G as D.
- Work 5 rnds of Diagonal Half & Half Square around Quad Colour Square beg with 4th rnd and using A as A and F as B.

SECTION 6

Finished measurements: 15 x 30.5cm (6 x 12in)

- Make 4 – Mitred Corner Rectangle: With foundation chain of 27, work 10 rows alternating rnds of A and B, beg with A.

SECTION 7

Finished measurements: 15 x 30.5cm (6 x 12in)

- Make 2 – Circle in a Square: Rnds 1-3 in G and rnds 4-5 in F.
- Make 2 – Circle in a Square: Rnds 1-3 in F and rnds 4-5 in G.

SECTION 8

Finished measurements: 30.5 x 30.5cm (12 x 12in)

- Make 6 in A – Classic Granny Version 1: 2 rnds in A.
- Make 6 in C – Classic Granny Version 1: 2 rnds in C.
- Make 6 in D – Classic Granny Version 1: 2 rnds in D.
- Make 2 squares as follows: With I, J.A.Y.go 9 squares together (two of each shade as seen in photo) and do not fasten off. Continuing with I, work 1 additional rnd in Granny Border pattern.

SECTION 9

Finished measurements: 15 x 30.5cm (6 x 12in)

- Make 2 – Basic Rectangle 1: With foundation ch of 26, work 5 rnds total with rnds 1-2 in G, rnds 3-4 in A and 5th rnd in D.

SECTION 10

Finished measurements: 30.5 x 30.5cm (12 x 12in)

- Make 8 - Diagonal Half & Half Square: 5 rnds with H as A and I as B.

SECTION 11

Finished measurements: 30.5 x 61cm (12 x 24in)

- Make 2 in C – Diamond: 5 rnds
- Make 2 in D – Diamond: 5 rnds
- Make 2 in E – Diamond: 5 rnds
- Make 2 in G – Half Rectangle Triangle: 9 rows.
- Make 2 in F – Half Rectangle Triangle: 9 rows
- Make 2 in A – Half Diamond Triangle 1: 4 rnds in A.

FINISHING

It is highly recommended to block prior to seaming using the preferred method from The Finishing: Rock the Block. Seam all the shapes together following the diagram and preferred seaming method (see The Finishing: All Together Now). Note: J.A.Y.go seaming is not recommended except as specified in Section 8.

SECTION 12 (BORDERS)

Note: The number of stitches to work in the first round of the Single Crochet Border must be accurate in order for each subsequent border to work.

* Single Crochet Border: With RS facing, join H with sl st to top-right corner of blanket. Ch 1 (does not count as st), 1 sc in same sp, work 167 sc evenly to next corner, 3 sc in corner, work 208 sc evenly down left side to next corner, 3 sc in corner, work 167 sc evenly across bottom to next corner, 3 sc in corner, work 208 sc evenly up right side to first corner, 2 sc in same sp as first st, join with sl st to first sc. Fasten off.
* Work 1 rnd Double Crochet Border in I.
* Work 1 rnd Granny Border: 1 rnd in H.
* Half circles border: With H and using instructions from the Heart, work 11 half circles across top and bottom edges with H. Work the first row with the wrong sides of the blanket facing.

About the Author

Julia Madill is a knit and crochet pattern designer, tech editor, and graphic artist. She loves sharing what she has learned in her 10+ years of experience in the yarn industry, providing others with the tools to create in their own style, voice and aesthetic. She lives in Toronto with her partner, two daughters, a cat named Pickles and a whole lot of yarn.

Photo Credit:Jennifer Rowsom Photography
www.jenniferrowsom.com

THANK YOU TO:

Austen, for unflinching support of all my hair-brained schemes.

Molly and Ivy, for their patience and understanding that playing with yarn is my job.

Vickie Howell, for all the encouragement and advice. You're my biggest cheerleader!

Michelle Lynch, crocheter extraordinaire, for her help testing and making samples.

Gayle Bunn, Svetlana Avrakh Nicole Winer, Emily Berney and Katherine Poole-Fournier, my designing women, who taught me so much about crochet pattern design.

Ame Verso, for taking a chance on my book idea.

All the editors, art directors, graphic designer and all staff at David & Charles who worked on this book.

Cascade Yarns for their generous yarn support for this book.

Index

A DAVID AND CHARLES BOOK

David and Charles is an imprint of David and Charles, Ltd
Suite A, Tourism House, Pynes Hill, Exeter, EX2 5WS

EU GPSR Authorised Representative:
Logos Europe, 9 rue Nicolas Poussin, 17000, La Rochelle, France
Email: Contact@logoseurope.eu

First published in the UK and USA in 2024

A catalogue record for this book is available from the British Library.

ISBN-13: 9781446310656 paperback
ISBN-13: 9781446312070 EPUB
ISBN-13: 9781446312100 PDF

This book has been printed on paper from approved suppliers and made from pulp from sustainable sources.

Printed in China through Asia Pacific Offset for:
David and Charles, Ltd
Suite A, Tourism House, Pynes Hill, Exeter, EX2 5WS

10 9 8 7 6 5 4 3

Publishing Director: Ame Verso
Managing Editor: Jeni Chown
Editor: Jessica Cropper
Tech Editor: Sam Winkler
Project Editors: Marie Clayton and Cheryl Brown
Head of Design: Anna Wade
Designer: Jo Webb
Pre-press Designer: Susan Reansbury
Crochet Chart Illustrations: Julia Madill
Art Direction: Sam Staddon
Photography: Jason Jenkins
Production Manager: Beverley Richardson

David and Charles publishes high-quality books on a wide range of subjects. For more information visit www.davidandcharles.com.

Share your makes with us on social media using #dandcbooks and follow us on Facebook and Instagram by searching for @dandcbooks.

Layout of the digital edition of this book may vary depending on reader hardware and display settings.